MW00583905

Praise for
Gita – A Timeless Guide for Our Time

"Gita is the ultimate guide for your spiritual journey.
A mesmerising translation of timeless wisdom.""

Deepak Chopra M.D.
#1 *New* York Times bestselling author of *The Healing Self*

"If a Westerner wants to experience firsthand why the
Bhagavad Gita has for centuries been heralded as one
of the world's most important texts, they could do no
better than to start their studies with Isaac Bentwich's
Gita – A Timeless Guide For Our Time. It so beautifully
captures the essence of this ancient Sanskrit text in a
way that modern thinkers everywhere can enjoy and
easily understand. I have not often recommended the
Bhagavad Gita to my western students—I will now."

Michael A. Singer
#1 *New* York Times bestselling author of *Untethered Soul*

"The Gita points beyond the deadening materialism of
modernity and shows how the greed, selfishness, and
destruction that threaten our existence can be overcome.
This exquisite, lyrical translation by Dr. Isaac Bentwich
is a great achievement. It will open a door to greater joy,
meaning, and purpose for all who read it."

Larry Dossey M.D.
New York Times bestselling author of *One Mind, Healing words*

"Isaac Bentwich's lyrical translation captures the heart and soul of the Bhagavad Gita. It is a testament to the timeless teachings of the ancient wisdom of India. Each verse and word of the Gita is so articulately compact that it unfolds piercing insights. It will awaken the hidden wisdom within you and create profound shifts every step of the way in your life. Each time I read a verse from this new translation, I am instantly inspired, renewed and reinvigorated."

Yogi Amrit Desai
One of the early pioneers who brought Yoga to the West
Award winning Author of *Yoga of Relationships* and *Love & Bliss*

"Translated in a poetic form matching the musical meter of the original Sanskrit text. Touches the heart and the soul by its poetic and musical rendition. Great translation of a great text."

Ravi Ravindra
Professor of Physics, Philosophy and Comparative Religion.
Renown author and translator of classic Yoga philosophy texts

"This is a totally unique translation of the Gita, unlike any other English translation I've seen. A moving, fresh, readable discourse, which puts the music back into the 'Song of the Lord' that is usually lost in translation, and is gender inclusive - which I believe Sri Krishna would also applaud. Highly recommended."

William Keepin, PhD
Author of *Belonging to God*

GITA
A TIMELESS GUIDE
FOR OUR TIME

GITA – A Timeless Guide for Our Time
Text © Copyright 2019 by Isaac Bentwich M.D.
Design © Copyright 2019 by Isaac Bentwich M.D.

All rights reserved.

Published by Harmonia Publications, www.harmonia.org.
4 Haruv Street, Zichron Yaakov, 3090530 Israel
To reorder please contact us at: bentwich@newgita.com.

Library of Congress Control Number (LCCN)

ISBN 978-965-7724-37-8

No part of this book may be reproduced without written permission.

Literal translation & transliteration: from 'The Bhagavad Gita'
by Swami Sivananda, Divine Life Society, 1944 www.dlshq.org.

Cover and Book Design: Isaac Bentwich and Nadav Shalev.

Gita is typeset in Mercury, Absara-Sans.

Cover photographs: used under license from iStock.com/Soubrette,
Nikada; and shutterstock/2265524729. All Rights Reserved.

Lotus photographs: Copyright Junjun, 2013, used under license from
Shutterstock.com. All Rights Reserved.

Frontispiece photograph: Krishna Arjuna Chariot, Rishikesh, India.
Photograph by Andrey Plis, used under license from Shutterstock.com.
All Rights Reserved.

Back cover: Author Photo by Gefen Bentwich, India, 2011.

First edition.
First printing: June 2019
10 9 8 7 6 5 4 3 2 1

GITA
A TIMELESS GUIDE
FOR OUR TIME

TRANSLATED BY
ISAAC BENTWICH M.D.

HARMONIA

"TODAY THE GITA

IS NOT ONLY MY BIBLE OR MY KORAN.

IT IS MORE THAN THAT, IT IS MY MOTHER.

WHEN I AM IN DIFFICULTY OR DISTRESS

I SEEK REFUGE IN HER BOSOM."

—

MAHATMA GANDHI

Dedicated
to the prince or princess within
each one of us; may the Gita help us, like the
Gita's Prince, greatest of archers, on our
individual inner journeys.

"*Om* is the bow,
The arrow is the Inner-Self,
The mark is said to be the Divine;
Attentively it should be penetrated,
Like an arrow lodged in the mark,
With the Divine – at One".

Mundaka Upanishad, II-4

TABLE OF CONTENTS

PREFACE

What is it about the Gita, that has captivated and inspired some of the world's most brilliant scientists, poets, thinkers and spiritual teachers, classic as well as contemporary? From Beethoven to Leonard Cohen; from Göethe to Carl Jung; from Schrödinger and Oppenheimer to Emerson and Thoreau; from Mahatma Gandhi to Deepak Chopra, Michael Singer and Eckhart Tolle. These, and so many others, found the Gita a source of Wisdom and inspiration.

Beethoven scribbled an inspiring verse from the Gita in his personal diary. Göethe said it is the book that enlightened him most in his whole life. Oppenheimer, who led the Manhattan Project, quoted a passage from the Gita when seeing the first Atomic detonation, and said the Gita is "the most beautiful philosophical song existing in any known tongue." And he should know: being the renaissance-man he was, he studied Sanskrit in order to read the Gita's original text, and kept a copy at his desk. Thoreau says in comparison to the Gita "our modern world and its literature seem puny and trivial, our Shakespeare seems sometimes youthfully green." Emerson finds it a "voice of an old intelligence, which in another age and climate had pondered and thus disposed of the same questions which exercise us." And Eckhart Tolle views it as "one of the greatest spiritual treasures of humanity."

Gita's still, clear voice – echoes the inner voice of your soul. It guides you on an inner-journey that will unleash your full potential, reminding you that your happiness does not depend on any teacher, guru or religion. It is a sacred ancient text that reveals the 'battlefield of the soul', the urgency of the struggle for peace in the soul, in which there is at once nothing and everything to do. An ancient inner-guide for happiness, meditation, and spiritual personal growth, which I believe is more relevant than ever in addressing our unique challenges today. The purpose of this translation is therefore to make the Gita more accessible and relevant to contemporary readers. A timeless guide for our time.

We're living in turbulent times. Times of unique opportunities and challenges, and of an intense 'battlefield', as it were, between matter and spirit. Our technology and science provide us ever growing comfort, security and abundance. But has it made mankind kinder? Less egotistical, less greedy, more content or happier? More accepting and open to others' faiths and beliefs? Is our breathtaking external material progress matched by the pace of inner-development and spiritual growth? We generate, and have access to, astounding amounts of knowledge. But is it bringing us, the family-of-man, closer to Wisdom? We've mapped the human genome and have made immense progress in medicine of the body; have we progressed much in our understanding and healing of Spirit and Soul?

And lastly, we face far less hardships and external dangers than our forefathers did; is it making our society warmer, more caring, tolerant and inclusive than it was? Is our democratic process imbued with a sufficiently vibrant moral sense, so as to ensure its legitimacy? Are our elected leaders today wiser than past ones, more inspiring in the ideals that motivate them and which they manifest?

The Gita is uniquely suited to helping us navigate these challenging times. It offers an urgent reminder that material progress and intellectual knowledge, no matter how impressive, do not beget inner spiritual maturity, and that the external challenges we face are ultimately a reflection of our internal 'battlefield of the soul' itself.

It is an 'inner-guide' written specifically for you. A guide, which echoes your inner-voice of Wisdom, gently reminding you truths your soul already knows. It offers you time-tested 'yardsticks' with which to assess, understand, and address the external challenges life brings. And, like a magic spiral stairway, as you read, and re-read this simple, profound discourse it keeps lifting you up higher, every time round. In the footsteps of giants before you, you're invited to this 'alchemy' of the Gita. It's timeless words of Wisdom empower you to do good in the world, and to be transformed in the process. To change the world around you, by first changing the world within.

* * *

There are many fine translations of the Gita, over two hundred translation in English alone, and hundreds of commentaries. I would like to offer the current translation, which I believe brings forth and makes accessible this 'inner-guide' aspect of the Gita, and its relevance to addressing the challenges of our time.

Specifically, the current translation is unique in three ways. First, it is the only translation that recreates in English, the mesmerizing melodiousness, meter and rhyme of the Sanskrit original. I believe this poetic form is imperative: allowing Gita's verses, like smooth 'pearls' of Wisdom, to melodiously roll around in your mind, and do their work. This helps awaken your intuition and avoid over-intellectualization, allowing you to gain direct experiential Wisdom, rather than mere intellectual knowledge.

Second, it is uniquely 'women empowering': Gita's text abounds in descriptions of the Spiritual Seeker, and of the Yogi – the ideal Enlightened person, both of which were previously translated as being male. The current translation is crafted such that it now 'speaks' directly to women and men alike, empowering women to 'reclaim' the Gita, in line with its inclusive, non sectarian message. I felt this is long overdue – our time, like never before, is blessed with women engaged in the practice and leadership of inner growth, spirituality and Yoga.

And third, it is written as a simple, practical guide for inner development, one which applies Gita's ancient Wisdom to our lives here and now. It crystallizes the key messages of each verse, as they apply to our time, while carefully 'peeling away' distracting layers of complex terminology and foreign culture.

In this respect, it is a very personal translation, one which echoes the impact that the Gita has had on my life. I'm a

Medical Doctor and a scientist, and have founded three life-science technology companies, leading revolutions in medicine, genomics, and environment conservation. I am also a longtime practitioner and teacher of Yoga and meditation.

Work on of this translation of the Gita spanned twelve years, and practicing Gita's teachings became enmeshed in my personal and professional life. The vision, innovation and scientific breakthroughs, which underlie each of the companies I founded – came through the 'alchemy' of long weeks of silent meditation. In the most concrete way – they are not mine. Gita became the 'toolbox' that carried and sustained me through these fascinating, unbelievably challenging journeys, and which transformed these challenges into powerful personal growth experiences. The current translation therefore seeks to share my passion for this magical 'toolbox' that the Gita offers, and its relevance to ordinary people, like you and me, who are living in this hectic, troubled, beautiful world and time of ours.

Each chapter is preceded by a short introductory text, with some personal musings on key messages of that chapter and on its relevance to your life and your inner-journey. These pre-chapter intro texts are 'vase-shaped', inviting us to open ourselves, as vessels, to accept the Wisdom of the Gita. The vase shape is also a reminder that these musings are merely 'water-from-the-well', not to be confused with the pure-source 'spring water' of the Gita itself.

A 'Yoga Philosophy Basics' introductory section briefly

defines Gita's key philosophical terms – I warmly recommend reading it first. And for those interested, the original Sanskrit text of each verse, its literal translation, and a word-by-word translation, are made available on the publisher's website; in the e-book version they are incorporated as hyperlinks. For more detail on the translation – see the 'About This Translation' annex.

To me, the magic of the Gita is its ability to convey the most profound, timeless philosophical truths – truths which transcend different beliefs and religions – with the laser-precision of a neurosurgeon's manual, in 'diagnosing' life's (and mind's) challenges, and 'prescribing' precise remedies for them. And yet doing so with mesmerizing melodiousness, and with utter simplicity, and life-and-death urgency of a dialogue taking place in the midst of a battlefield, thereby emphasizing introspection rather than intellectualization. I hope you'll find the above approaches I've taken support these qualities of the Gita, and make its inspiring timeless message more accessible and relevant.

* * *

For over two and a half millennia, the Gita (formally Bhagavad Gita, meaning Divine Song) has been one of the world's most trusted guides for happiness, meditation, and spiritual inner growth.

The text is a dialogue between master and disciple. The disciple is Indian prince Arjuna, a courageous warrior and a highly evolved spiritual seeker, called to fight a defensive battle against vicious family members who are out to kill him. Shaken by the moral dilemma, Arjuna shirks from fighting, and seeks counsel of his teacher, Krishna, who is also his friend and charioteer, and ...no less than God incarnate. It is in this harsh battlefield setting, that the master, Krishna, leads prince Arjuna from the worldly starting point of the prince's despondency, to a captivating, brilliantly clear account of the meaning of life, the source of suffering, and the paths to happiness and self-fulfillment.

In the translation, I let Arjuna and Krishna – simply be the Prince and the Master. For the Gita is truly a book about you, and your everyday 'battlefields'. You are the Princess or Prince, and the book is the most intimate of dialogues, a dialogue with your 'inner-voice' of Wisdom, and any wise masters you meet on your journey, who echo that voice.

The path charted is that of Yoga in its broadest sense. Like a majestic lotus flower gradually unfolding its petals, the Gita presents three complementary paths, which you meet on your inner quest. The journey begins with the *Action Path*, which teaches you how to transform your ego-driven worldly activity into selfless, compassionate altruism. The *Devotion Path* then develops your emotional intelligence and intuition, lifting you to realize with awe, Spirit which permeates Matter, and the Divine beauty and Unity of the world that surrounds you. Finally, the *Wisdom Path* leads you, through introspection, philosophical inquiry and meditation – to experience this Unity and Beatitude as your true identity, previously veiled by egoism.

The physical Yoga postures and exercises, a familiar and trusted part of our life for many of us, are enmeshed into these three paths, and serve as wonderful facilitators for them. These exercises, with their gentle discipline and quiet awareness, help you transform activeness of body and mind into a more relaxed, inward in-tuned state. And they provide a 'taste' of the serenity within, which you gradually learn to identify as your true Inner-Self.

Yoga practice has touched the lives of tens of millions in the West (thirty five million in the U.S. alone, up from twenty million four years ago). Many Yoga practitioners are content with obtaining a toned, flexible body. That is fine. But for those interested – the real benefit of Yoga, as articulated by the Gita, is a profound inner-change.

All of the masters who have brought Yoga to the West, advocate Gita's central importance to the practice of Yoga. Yogananda said "Gita is India's scripture of scriptures, the most beloved scripture of India, the one book that all masters depend upon." And B.K.S. Iyengar, broadly recognized for introducing Yoga to the Western world, proclaimed the Gita as "the most important authority on Yoga philosophy."

* * *

I first encountered the Gita thirty-two years ago, in a Yoga teachers' training course, and ...really hated it! Being very much connected to my Jewish roots, I was not at all attracted to Indian mythology, and to this somewhat bizarre dialogue. I dozed off in the lectures, joked about the Indian quirks, and waited impatiently for the classes to be over. Yet, it is the Gita, that eventually became my great Love, and opened a door for a profound change in my life.

Like the Gita's Prince, we all struggle, in our different ways, to find balance and satisfaction in our lives, as we tackle life's challenges. The materialistic world we live in often deepens our sense of thirst – a thirst for happiness, for satisfaction, for meaning and for harmony. And yet, these are at times so elusive. One moment you are happy, and in the next moment your world trembles and shatters. At times, you have 'everything', and yet still fail to find satisfaction in your life. At other times, your daily struggle itself seems almost too difficult to bear.

The Gita invites you to join the Prince, as he has his 'friendly chat with God'. You often find yourself asking the same questions he does, and the answers provided, surprising at times, stimulate you to think. The dialogue masterfully portrays both explanations for your inner turmoil, as well as paths to changing it from its very core. The paths leading there, the Gita reminds us, depend not on some acclaimed Guru or therapist, nor are they to be found in some foreign religion or philosophy. Rather, they are in your heart and in your very hands.

The way is difficult and demanding, for it requires a fundamental change of the way you regard yourself and the world around you. Like an infant, flexing its muscles for the first time, the Gita invites you to learn and practice how to 'flex' your mind and your heart: how to act, how to think and feel, and how to talk. But such fundamental change is not theoretical. It is indeed attainable, at least to a degree, here and now, for each and every one of us.

The text itself is not easy. It deals with existential questions, and its approach is direct and uncompromising. Each of us will find in the text, passages that we find clear and appealing, and others that are not. We are advised to leave those passages which do not move us, and focus on those that do.

Remind yourself to be patient. Like any wisdom scripture, the Gita is meant for slow iterative reading and study, preferably combined with meditation. Find what works best for you. Reading a bit when you feel like it. Or perhaps read a chapter a day, or repeat the same chapter every day for a week. Following the reading, sit and meditate (or meditate in motion), perhaps reflecting in your meditation on a verse that appeals to you. Then let it 'percolate' in your mind and in your heart throughout your day's activity, and your interactions with others, finding and deepening its relevance to your life. When possible, get together with like-minded others, to meditate together and to share; such gatherings are blessed. And seek the company of such fellow seekers, even if remotely – sharing verses that move you, and sharing inner-journey's difficulties and triumphs. Bit by bit, through such reading and practice, things become clearer. In the silence of meditation, allow the messages of the text echo within, gradually affecting and merging into your daily life. Allow them, like pure water drops patiently pounding against rock, to melt away, bit by bit, the walls of habits, which keep you away from your true Self.

*   *   *

Laboring on the translation of this magical book has been the greatest treasure for me. Spanning twelve long years, it became enmeshed in my life, and served as an anchor, a mast and a compass in troubled seas. In magical early morning hours before dawn, before the workday's 'race' begins, and in periods of silent meditation retreats in the Galilee and at the foothills of the Himalayas.

And now it is in your hands, inviting you to embark on an exciting journey to a destination which is both far and very near, the most important of all journeys, perhaps the only journey there really is: the inward journey, to your own Self.

The Gita has been an abundant source of Light in my life. I pray that it will be so in your life as well.

Isaac Bentwich M.D., Spring 2019

YOGA PHILOSOPHY BASICS

The following is a summary of fifteen key concepts of Vedanta, Yoga's underlying philosophy. The original Sanskrit terms are in brackets. Gita's entire text is largely a detailed description of these.

The Divine (Brahman)
Under the infinite variability in our world, says Vedanta philosophy, there exists a perfect, unchanging, indivisible unity, which is not perceived by the senses, nor by mind and thought. This unity is called the Divine (also referred to as Reality, Absolute, Supreme, or Consciousness).

Inner-Self (Atman)
A 'fragment', as it were, of the Divine, which exists in every one of us, and which is the very core of your being, your true essence.

Nature's-Veil (Maya)
The visible world, with its manifold details, hides as it were, the Divine, the unity-within-all. This 'veiling' of the Divine-in-all is referred to as Nature's-Veil, or Creation's-Illusion.

Ignorance (Avidya)
Mesmerized by Nature's-Veil, you falsely identify yourself with ego, body and mind, rather than with your true Divine

essence, Inner-Self. This 'forgetfulness' of who you are – is Ignorance.

Action-Bonds (Karma), Death-Rebirth Cycle (Samsara)
In Ignorance, in your mistaken identification with ego, your actions cause Action-Bonds, Karma, which bind you to their results. The present is shaped by your past deeds, and your current actions shape the future. This is the seemingly endless Death-Rebirth Cycle.

Wisdom (Jnana), Liberation (Moksha)
Wisdom is knowing your true Divine nature. Your current false conviction and identification 'I am this ego, this limited, mortal body and mind' is replaced by the unshakable, non-intellectual realization: 'I am the Divine, indivisible, infinite'. The dawning of this Wisdom in your heart – is Liberation (or Enlightenment, Illumination). It dispels the Ignorance that never was, as light dispels a shadow-figure, which you took to be real. When Wisdom dawns, actions are no longer ego-driven, and hence no longer bind you. This is life's ultimate goal.

Nature's-Facets (Gunas):
Pure (Satva), Active (Rajas), Dull (Tamas)
The three Nature-Facets, or Traits – Pure, Active and Dull – are three aspects or forces of nature, of Nature's-Veil. Training your mind to be ever aware of these, helps you realize it is nature that is acting, not you.

Calling, Duty (Dharma)

We each have our own Calling, or natural Duty, reflecting our temperament. Pursuing it wholeheartedly and selflessly is an important key to your happiness and to Liberation.

Yoga

Yoga (literally: union, integration) is the sum of all paths of inner development, the goal of which is to realize and experience your Divine true Inner-Self, and thereby live a harmonious life. Description of the different Yoga paths, is the subject of the Gita.

Meditation (Dhyana)

Meditation is a method of inner practice, central to Yoga, for transcending mind's noisy thoughts. Through meditation, you gradually go beyond intellect, ego and emotions. Experiencing, at least partially, our true, Divine, Inner-Self.

PART ONE

Path of Action

PREFACE TO CHAPTER ONE

Our Gita journey begins with a dramatic backdrop. The dialogue we're about to hear – a dialogue which investigates
life's most profound questions, takes place in what
appears to be the least likely of settings. Not in
serene nature or in academia's lofty halls, but in
the chaotic, messy midst of a violent battlefield.
Which, when you come to think of it, is actually
perfect. You see, this is not a story about some his-
toric battle in some far-away land. It is a story about you.
You are the Princess, or Prince, and this is your story, and
the story of your ever-changing daily 'battlefields'. Those at
work, in relationships, in parenting, in creativity, in spiritual
search, and in attempting to balance all these. For it is in the
midst of your daily 'battlefields' that your heart truly opens
to change, to inner growth, and that you seek wisdom. It
is the real story, pulsating underneath, and manifest-
ing through, all of your life's dramas, big and small.
Gita's dialogue between Prince and Master –
echoes your own dialogue with the inner
voice of your soul, and any wise masters
you meet on your path. It guides you
on an inner-journey that will unleash your full potential.

CHAPTER ONE

The Prince's Sorrow

PRINCE:

O Master, pray halt my chariot,
Between the armies, plainly in sight;
Let me behold them, bold warriors,
With whom I must battle and fight. [21,22]

Pray let me observe and know them,
Men gathered, desiring war;
Their leader – my evil uncle,
Dark-hearted he is and abhorred. [23]

The Master then drove that chariot — none grander ever
seen since; and halting between the armies, said:
"Behold the two armies, O Prince".

And in both armies the Prince saw — so many dear
faces he knew: fathers and sons, uncles and in-laws —
grandfathers, teachers, and many friends too. When he
saw them, thus pitted against one another — all these
dear friends and kinsfolk; anguished, filled with deep pity
— he turned to the Master and spoke:

PRINCE:
Master, Master, now as I see them,
These relatives, eager to fight;
My body trembles, mouth parching,
Limbs fail at this horrible sight. [28,29]

My faithful bow from my hand slips,
My knees are soft, hairs stand on end;
And I see such omens, Master,
See no good, in killing these men. [30,31]

What need I victory, O Master?
What use have I for dominion?
When all these many dear others,
Sons, fathers, uncles and brothers, [32,33]

For whose sake alone, O Master
Earthly pleasures we would enjoy;
Risk their wealth, their very own lives,
In this bloody, despicable ploy. [34]

How can I strike them, O Master?
Never! I'd rather be slain!
Not for ruling the heavens,
Less so for mere dominion of men. [35]

Revered, wise merciful Master,
Please counsel me, answer me, pray;
How can we hope to be happy,
If our very own family we slay? [36]

Though evil, worst of the wicked,
If we kill them – greater's our sin;
Dare we spill the blood that unites us?
Is there glory – slaying one's kin? [37]

Darkened are their hearts, Master,
Their intelligence – blinded by greed;
See no wrong killing family,
In treason – they see no misdeed. [38]

Shun we not this crime, Master,
We, who family ruin clearly see?
Brother-murder, most vile, it is!
Has ambition got hold of me? [39,45]

Rather let my evil relatives,
Weapons in hand, let them attack;
I'd rather be slain in battle,
Let them strike – I will not strike back. [46]

Thus spoke the Prince in the battlefield midst — casting
his bow and his arrows; sat down in his chariot's seat —
mind fraught with the deepest of sorrows.

"**ABANDON ALL THOUGHT OF THE CONSEQUENCE, AND MAKE THE EVENT EQUAL, WHETHER IT TERMINATE IN GOOD OR EVIL; FOR SUCH AN EQUALITY IS CALLED YOGA.**"

—

Gita quote, from diary of
Ludwig Van Beethoven

Gita's second chapter begins with the Prince shaken to his core:
repulsed by violence, and deadlocked by terrible external
circumstances and an impossible dilemma. And we are
naturally moved by, and identify with, his noble re-
volt and his anguish – who wouldn't? Note how
beautiful and fitting it is, that it's only after he
breaks down and humbly asks for help – "guide me
Master, what aught I do, I'm your disciple, show me
the way" – that he is really ready to receive guidance. The
Master's anti-climatic, serene response, delivered "wearing
the faintest of smiles", shocks us, as it must have shocked the
Prince. Don't be fooled by life's external dramas – says the Gita
– rather look within to find the source of your joy and suffering. Recognize that life inevitably brings recurring waves
of such joy and sorrow. Learn to address them by training
your mind. Your real battle is not with external enemies,
it is an inner 'battle' and an inner quest, to find inner
peace in the face of life's ever enfolding drama:
"Senses contacting their objects cause feelings
— of heat and cold, joy and pain to evince;
they come and they go, they never last
long — you must learn to bravely endure them, O Prince."

CHAPTER TWO

Yoga of Wisdom

To him, tearful-eyed, despondent — who was thus
overcome by grieving; the Master, slayer-of-evil — then
turned and sternly spoke, saying:

MASTER:
Is this hour of battle, O Prince,
A time for scruples and qualms?
Mere cravers of heaven shun them,
More so you, who Freedom would find. [2]

What is this debilitation?
Stand up firm, Prince, resolve to fight!
Timidity is beneath you,
Shake off, this weakness of heart! [3]

PRINCE:

These relatives are noble, Master,
Worthy of highest esteem;
How greet I them with arrows?
O Master, so wrong it all seems. [4]

Why, blood guilt befouls and poisons
All joys and pleasures, if they're dead;
Prefer I indeed to spare them, and
Forever – eat beggar's bread. [5]

To vanquish or be defeated,
Which is worst, I hardly can tell;
In enemy ranks – stand my own,
Slaying them, I'd wish death alone. [6]

A veil of pity routs my heart,
Mind's dark: Where does my duty lay?
Guide me, Master, what ought I do?
I'm your disciple, show me the way. [7]

Not all the riches of Earth, no,
Nor attaining gods' heavenly throne;
Can ease the grief that numbs my senses,
Remove this sorrow I've known. [8]

Thus spoke the brave warrior Prince — conqueror-of-sleep, master-of-will; "I shall not fight!" he added — and then spoke no more and was still. Then, to him, between the two armies — disconsolate by these tormenting trials; the Master, ruler-of-senses, spoke — wearing the faintest of smiles:

MASTER:
You speak words of wisdom, O Prince,
But your sorrow is in vain;
For the truly Wise never mourn,
Neither the living nor the slain. [11]

There was never a time we were not,
Me, or you, or these enemy kings;
Nor can there be any future
In which we ever cease being. [12]

This body's Dweller, throughout life,
Wears bodies of child, youth, old man;
At death – He but dons another,
The Wise grieve not, they understand. [13]

Senses contacting their objects cause feelings
Of heat and cold, joy and pain to evince;
They come 'n they go, they never last long,
You must learn to bravely endure them, O Prince! [14]

A serene spirit accepts
Pleasure and pain even-mindedly;
Know, O Prince, that it alone is
Worthy of immortality. [15]

The non-existent cannot come into being,
Nor can That which exists ever cease to be;
Knowers of Truth know what Is, what Is-Not,
They're Seers of the highest Reality. [16]

Know That, Reality – which is
All pervading, imperishable;
No one can cause destruction of
That which is indestructible. [17]

These bodies, O Prince, are all mortal,
Given to sorrow and blight;
Body's Dweller and Master is
Eternal – therefore you must fight! [18]

Mistaken are those thinking that
Inner-Self can kill or be put to death;
How can it possibly slay, and
Who'd kill it, take its life's breath? [19]

Know Inner-Self as timeless,
No beginning or ending it has;
Deathless, birthless, ever unchanged,
How can it die the body's death? [20]

One who Realizes Inner-Self
As birthless, deathless, unchanging;
How shall one like this kill, Prince,
Or possibly cause any killing? [21]

The body sheds worn-out garments
And wears a new garb in its stead;
Body's Dweller, Inner-Self – dons a
New body when an old one is shed. [22]

By wind it cannot be dried,
Nor can it be wetted by water;
By weapons it cannot be cut,
And will not be burnt by fire. [23]

Such is the Inner-Self: not burnt,
Not wounded, not dried, not wet;
Innermost element, Changeless,
Of every being, every event. [24]

This Inner-Self is changeless,
Perceived not by senses or thought;
Knowing this truth – reflect, O Prince:
Clearly you should grieve not. [25]

But even if the Inner-Self,
Could be born or die – so you thought;
Why, Prince – even if this was so,
Thinking clearly you should grieve not. [26]

Re-birth is certain for the dead,
Death certain for those who are born;
That which is inevitable,
Surely, Prince, mustn't be mourned. [27]

Before birth all beings aren't manifest here,
Birth to death – to our senses they're plain;
After death, again they are un-manifest,
What ever for do you grieve for or pain? [28]

Some witnessed Inner-Self's glory,
Some speak of it beyond their grasp;
Others, know of it by hearsay,
And but Ignorance do they clasp. [29]

Inner-Self dwells, ever deathless,
Within all bodies ever born;
Therefore, Prince, there is no one, whom
You should lament for or mourn. [30]

Even your natural-born Calling,
Your role as Leader and Warrior;
Behooves you to fight, wavering not, for
None is nobler than righteous war. [31]

Die, and you win heaven above,
Conquer – earth is for your delight;
Stand up firm, therefore, O Prince,
And resolve to do battle and fight! [37]

Establish, firm, your equal-mind,
To gain and loss, pleasure and pain;
Equal-minded – go to battle,
Act thus – and you cannot sin. [38]

I've taught you now the Wisdom Path,
To Knowledge of Inner-Self 'twill lead;
Now hear how through the Action Path,
From bondage of actions you're freed. [39]

Action Path's practice cannot harm
Nor can it be wasted, you see;
Even a little diligence here, from
Death-Rebirth Cycle sets you free. [40]

The Action Yogi practices,
Focuses the mind, dispassionate;
Unlike poor souls, whose endless
Thoughts – gush forth, indiscriminate. [41]

Fools, with their flowery speech,
Joy quoting Scriptures, to the letter;
Blind to their deeper meaning, Prince,
Indeed, they do not know better. [42]

Craving worldly and heaven's rewards,
Pleasure and power they'd attain;
Teaching rituals that but bind them
To birth-and-death over again. [43]

Those craving pleasure and power
Are forcefully drawn by such talk;
They gain no focused dispassion,
Which leads man to union with God. [44]

Three Nature-Facets act in and around us:
Pure, Active, Dull – learn to master them, Prince;
Free from opposite-pairs and thoughts-of-possession
Be Pure, be established in Inner-Self's peace. [45]

To the Illumined Seer, Prince,
Scriptures are superfluous indeed;
Even as when land is flooded
The reservoir is of no need. [46]

You have the right to work, O Prince,
But not to the fruits this work breeds;
Never work for fruits of your labor
Nor to laziness ever concede. [47]

Abandon clinging to your work's results,
Act always heart-united with the Divine;
True Yoga is the art of maintaining,
In success and failure an even-mind. [48]

Anxious work, for results, is inferior to
Selfless, Action-Yoga work, expecting none;
Establish yourself in Yoga-of-Action!
Wretched are those who seek prize for work
done. [49]

Every action, good or bad,
Performed hoping its fruits to enjoy;
Forms Action-Bonds, shackles of Karma,
Their outcome you cannot avoid.

|

But if you act not desiring a thing
Why then your actions form no bond;
Devote yourself to Yoga, Prince: selfless
Skilled-action, sagely performed. [50]

In the peace of calm surrender
The Wise renounce their actions' fruit;
Thus they're freed from re-birth's bonds,
Beyond good 'n bad, Freedom Absolute. [51]

When the intellect's false notion
"This body I am" – has cleared through;
Then, dry intellectual reasonings
Will be of no interest to you. [52]

Now, your intellect's perplexed by
Analyzing what Scriptures teach;
When it rests calm, focused inwards,
Inner-Self's Unity – you'll reach. [53]

PRINCE:
Master, what describes one who is
Established in the Absolute? How
does an Illumined Yogi speak? How
does one walk? How does one sit? [54]

MASTER:
One who has known Inner-Self's bliss
No longer craves anything at all;
Tormenting desires all renounced, Prince,
- O what an Illumined soul. [55]

Stirred not by pain, nor seeking joy,
Free from attachments, big or small;
Free from anger, free from all fears,
- O what an Illumined soul. [56]

Meets fortune and does not rejoice,
Nor saddened when misfortune befalls;
Bonds of attachment all broken,
– O what an Illumined soul. [57]

Withdrawing the senses at will,
By sights and sounds no longer controlled;
Like a tortoise, withdrawing its limbs,
– O what an Illumined soul. [58]

Abstainers flee craved objects,
Desires carried in their mind;
When entering Reality, O Prince,
One leaves all passions behind. [59]

Even the mind of a wise person,
A mind which clearly knows the way;
By the senses, so turbulent,
Can be violently dragged 'n sway. [60]

But the Yogi recollects the mind,
Pulling the senses under control;
Fixing the mind on Me, Divine,
- O what an Illumined soul. [61]

Thinking of sights and scents and sound,
To these sense-objects binds your mind;
Grow attached – addiction you seed,
Fight addiction – anger 'twill breed, [62]

Anger – and you confuse your mind,
Mind confused – experience you forget;
Experience gone – discernment you lose,
Life's goal you miss – if you lose that. [63]

One who's free from 'likes' and 'dislikes'
Amidst all sense-objects – treads safe;
Finding peaceful joy, O Prince,
Within one's own Inner-Self. [64]

All sorrows and pains are destroyed,
Dissolving into that clear peace;
The tranquil-minded intellect
Soon becomes established in Bliss. [65]

Rampant mind – knows not Inner-Self,
How can it then Meditate, Prince?
Can there be peace without Meditation,
Or happiness when there's no peace? [66]

As violent winds drift a boat,
From its course they drag it askew;
So do 'winds-of-senses' whirl the mind,
Clouding reason and judgment too. [67]

Praised be one who can calm the senses,
Bringing them fully under control;
Their sense-object turmoil – restrain,
– O what an Illumined soul. [68]

Silent mind is awake to Inner-Self, which
Is but darkness to the Ignorant's sight;
The Ignorant to sense-life are awake,
Daylight for them, a Seer's dark night. [69]

One truly knows peace when even desires
Flooding the mind its peace cannot perturb;
Like wild rivers gushing into calm ocean
Yet ocean's tranquility they never disturb. [70]

When desires are fully abandoned,
Only then – does one know true peace;
Living without any longing,
Free from ego and pride, O Prince. [71]

This is the Illumined state, Prince,
One's delusion – forever is gone;
Even when body dies – one Lives,
With the Divine, Absolute – at One. [72]

Gita teaches the art of living life wisely. And so, our journey
starts from the most pragmatic aspect of our lives – Action.
Our lives are so immersed in Action (and more so in
re-action) that we tend to be mesmerized by our
current drama-of-the-day, and therefore miss the
bigger picture, the dynamics of Action itself. Our
actions (and thoughts!) are so completely driven by
Ego that a false conviction sets in that we *are* Ego, and
that there's nothing we can do about it. Gita's Action Path,
and this chapter specifically, help you better understand the
nature of Action, empowering you to transform your activity
from ego-driven actions and thoughts that shackle you, to selfless ones that gradually set you free. You cannot avoid activity, says the Gita. But make sure you work selflessly. Work
for work's sake alone. We each have our life's-work, our
Calling. Find and embrace your life's Calling. Enjoy work
itself, thereby enjoying the present moment. It is futile
to obsess over the past, or fret about work's future
results – says the Gita – "but one who works,
unattached — senses and mind held under
rein; merits highest regard, O Prince
— this is true Yoga-of-Action.

CHAPTER THREE

Yoga of Action

PRINCE:

But Master, if you assert that
Wisdom is better than Action;
Then why do you tell me to do
Such dreadful deeds of destruction? [1]

Your words seem contradictory,
Confusion they stir in my mind;
Tell me one certain way, Master,
By which one may reach the Divine. [2]

MASTER:

Seekers of enlightenment, in this world, Prince,
Have two paths, for two personality types:
Wisdom Path for the mature, reflective,
And Selfless Action for those who're still active. [3]

Non-action can never achieve
The action-less state on its own;
Nor can perfection be attained
By renouncing action alone. [4]

No one can rest for a moment
From action of body and thought;
Nature's-Facets compel us to act
Hence our life with action is fraught. [5]

One who curbs action of body
But harbors desires in thought;
Is a deluded hypocrite,
Wisdom in this – there is not. [6]

But one who works, unattached,
Senses and mind held under rein;
Merits highest regard, O Prince,
This is true Yoga-of-Action. [7]

Action surpasses inaction,
Act, from natural Duty don't abstain;
Why even your very own body,
Without action you cannot sustain. [8]

This world by its actions is chained,
Save when action's performed as prayer;
Perform all acts as prayer, therefore,
And for action's fruits never care. [9]

At creation's dawn, each soul was given
A natural-born Calling, its own ordained part;
'Your wishes be granted' said the Creator,
'If your Calling's Duty you perform, pure of
heart'. [10]

Pursuing your Calling honors God,
Upon you – God's light will shine;
By honoring one another,
One attains to – the Divine. [11]

Please the Lord, pursue your Calling,
And He will answer your prayers;
And forget not to always give thanks,
For enjoying God's bounty and grace. [12]

The righteous eat what God provides,
A grateful prayer in their hearts;
But those who cook for stomach's greed,
Know this surely on vice do they feed. [13]

All life is nourished by food, and
All food – by God's rain is sustained;
Rain – is provided through prayer, and
Prayer – is by Action ingrained. [14]

Action stems from the Creator,
Eternal, forever unchanged;
Know therefore that the good Lord,
In this cycle forever remains. [15]

One who neglects one's ordained part
In this wheel of action and prayer;
Know this, Prince – in vain is such life
Of wasteful vice, lust and desire. [16]

But when in Inner-Self, one finds
Delight, satisfaction and peace;
One is then no longer compelled
To act, nor anything to achieve. [17]

Whether one acts or acts not,
What has one to lose or to gain?
No longer desires or craves,
Needs nothing, depends on no man. [18]

Perform then your Calling's Duty,
But do so always – unattached;
Working, unconcerned by outcome,
You attain the Supreme, at last. [19]

King Janaka, like many others,
Attained Liberation this way;
Like them, act, setting example
Of performing one's Duty well. [20]

All that a great person says or does,
Others will always imitate;
Blindly they follow the example,
Which this person illustrates. [21]

Learn from My example, O Prince,
Observe Me closely, the Divine;
I work though there's nothing I need
For heavens and earth are all mine. [22]

Had I stopped working tirelessly
Mankind would follow my lead;
Their work – they would all neglect,
Decay and world ruin would breed. [23,24]

The Ignorant work – craving results,
Let the Wise – work for world's gain;
Thereby they set an example
Of performing one's Duty ordained. [25]

Minds of the Ignorant hunger for action,
Not to confuse them the Wise must take care;
Better they perform their Duty for its fruits,
Let the Wise set example – working as prayer. [26]

Nature's-Facets cause all action 'n thought,
Understanding this, Prince, is key;
Man, in dark Ignorance, thinks:
"I am the doer, the actor is me". [27]

"When senses see sights or hear sounds
'Tis but Nature's-Facets interacting";
One who's Wise – Knows this for certain
And so is never bound by acting. [28]

Fools act, deluded by Nature's-Facets,
Fruits of their actions they crave;
Let not the Wise confuse them, better
They work – from idling be saved. [29]

Shake off this Ignorance fever that blinds you,
Pledge all your actions as prayer to the Divine;
Free from hope and ego stand up then and fight!
Inner-Self, O Prince, firmly fixed in your mind. [30]

Those steadfast in this My practice,
From Karma, the bonds of their deeds,
Through faithful, divine conviction,
Know this, Prince, will surely be freed. [31]

But those who despise these teachings,
Always carp, yet practice them not;
Lacking Wisdom and discernment, verily
Their own doom they've brought. [32]

All creatures, even the Wise,
Act, driven by habits engrained;
Seemingly then, what use is it
These tendencies – to try and restrain? [33]

Indeed 'tis Senses' nature to be
By some objects drawn, repulsed by some;
But know that through practiced restraint
Born-tendencies are all overcome. [34]

Adhere then to your natural-born Calling,
Restraining the senses as best as you can;
Better imperfectly follow your Calling
Than perfectly tackle that of another man. [35]

PRINCE:
But Master, what causes one
Not wishing it – to do evil?
Where one seems compelled, as it were,
To act – against one's own will? [36]

MASTER:

Desire and desire-bred anger,
From Activeness' Facet – both arose;
All-destructive, insatiable, Prince,
Know them well, your timeless foes. [37]

Smoke hides fire, dust hides a mirror,
Embryo by uterus is veiled;
Know that by desire, O Prince,
Inner-Self is hidden, concealed. [38]

Desire, arch-enemy of the Wise,
Obscures Inner-Self in its blaze;
Can fuel poured onto a fire,
Ever quench – fire's thirsty craze? [39]

The senses, mind and intellect,
Are its seat and its very fuel;
Body's Dweller it bewilders,
And Wisdom – it veils and fools. [40]

Control the senses first, therefore,
Then slay this evil thing, desire;
It blocks Realization of Inner-Self,
The Highest – to which you aspire. [41]

Senses are higher than sense-objects,
Mind over senses, Intellect over mind;
But Inner-Self is highest – it is their
Source – they're under Its command. [42]

Therefore let your Divine-nature, Inner-Self,
Restrain your mind, Prince, your lower human
one; Then smite your elusive enemy, desire!
Within, not without – the real battle is won. [43]

PREFACE TO CHAPTER FOUR

Gita's fourth chapter discusses Action and its relation to Wisdom. Action and stillness are in the mind – says the Gita – learn to connect with your inner stillness. You're active when your thoughts are racing, or your emotions are turbulent, even if you're sitting perfectly still in serene nature. And you may find, and cultivate, a peaceful serenity within, even while your body is engaged in its daily activities, in the midst of hectic surroundings. Those practicing Yoga postures and Flow, or Chi movement techniques, will find these concepts very familiar, and synergistic to their practice: working with the micro-movement within a pose, and cultivating the 'stillness-in-movement'. It is an 'alchemy', which harnesses action, to reach a stillness within. Practicing selfless, mindful action leads to a dawning of Wisdom in your heart: a growing realization that you are not this limited body-mind, a realization which transcends our current ego-driven state. You start your journey, dominated by action and addicted to it. And then gradually, through selfless-action and mindful awareness, "every action [becomes] a prayer and an offering — and action itself then dissolves and is gone."

CHAPTER FOUR

Renunciation through Wisdom

MASTER:

I taught this Yoga immortal
To the ancient sages at first;
They passed it on in succession
Until throughout time it was lost. [1,2]

This Yoga, ancient and secret,
Through its practice death you transcend;
I teach it now to you, O Prince,
My faithful disciple and friend. [3]

PRINCE:

The ancient sages, O Master,
Were all born – long before you;
You say you taught this Yoga first,
How can I accept this as true? [4]

MASTER:

You and I both, O brave Prince, have
Lived through countless lives before;
I know each one of these clearly,
While you recall no lives of yore. [5]

My birth, is but an appearance, Prince,
I am the Immortal, this whole world My design;
Master of Nature, of Creation's-Illusion,
Which has created this body of Mine. [6]

Time and again I don body,
When good wanes, evil prevails;
In every age I return to
Guard virtue and the wicked assail. [7,8]

One who thus knows Me correctly,
Seeming birth and action sublime;
Is not reborn when shedding body,
But comes to Me, the Divine. [9]

Many've in Me taken refuge,
Freed from anger, from fear and lust;
Purged by Divine Wisdom's fire,
Which burns all past traits into dust. [10]

Whatever one wishes – I grant
If to Me, Divine, one turns in prayer;
Any path one takes is My path,
For all paths, O Prince, do lead there. [11]

Most long for worldly successes
And so pray to this or that god;
Such success mundane is in truth
Quite easily gained in this world. [12]

The four Social Classes reflect
Nature's-Facets and Karma, past deeds;
I, Divine, am beyond action,
Though I'm the creator of these. [13]

Action's fruits I desire not,
Hence action won't taint Me, Divine;
One is not bound by one's actions,
When grasping this nature of Mine. [14]

The ancient Wise freedom seekers
Safely acted, for this they knew;
In the spirit of these Seers,
You should perform your actions too. [15]

What is action, what is inaction?
This confuses even the Wise;
I'll teach you their nature and thus
Above Birth-Death's Cycle you'll rise. [16]

You must know what is inaction,
What action's good, what's to be banned;
The true nature of action, O Prince,
Is most difficult to understand. [17]

Action within inaction, and
Inaction that action contains;
One who Sees these is Wise, O Prince,
Body may act yet one is at peace. [18]

All one's actions are selfless now,
One's deeds – without any desire;
The bonds of these actions consumed,
Burnt by Divine Wisdom's fire. [19]

No longer attached to action's fruits,
Needs nothing, has no craving thoughts;
Ever content in Inner-Self,
Body active – yet one acts not. [20]

Hoping gone, craving abandoned,
Tightly reining body and mind;
Ego's good deeds will still bind you,
Such egoless acts do not bind. [21]

Content with what God provided,
Even-minded in joy and in pain;
One acts, is not bound by actions,
Free from envy, from loss or gain. [22]

To one who is unattached, Liberated,
Whose mind is in Wisdom established, enthroned;
Every action is a prayer and an offering,
And action itself then dissolves and is gone. [23]

The Divine is the ritual,
The offering given – Divine;
Divine is one who serves it to,
The sacrificial fire – Divine.
|
One who in every action,
Unceasingly sees the Divine;
This Divine, Supreme-Reality,
Verily, one will indeed find. [24]

Many Yoga Wisdom-Practices
To the Divine lead the way;
Some Yogis' path is simply prayer,
To their chosen god – they pray.

|

Others meditate, seek to Realize the oneness
Of Inner-Self with the Absolute, the Divine;
They 'burn', as-it-were, their own Inner-Self, by
The 'holy flame' of this Reality Sublime. [25]

Some withdraw, deprive their senses
From contact with all sounds 'n scenes;
'Burning', as though, their senses, by
The 'flame' of their Self-discipline.

|

Others let awareness and senses roam free,
Seeing only Divine in all that's around them;
The world's every sound and sight they thus 'offer',
'Burnt', as it were, by their senses' 'holy flame'. [26]

Some renounce senses completely,
Sense activity they wish to 'maim';
Inner-Self Wisdom 'kindles', as though
Their practiced-control's 'holy flame'. [27]

For some Wisdom-Practice is giving of alms,
Possessions renounced and all left behind;
Others' Wisdom Practice is strict discipline:
Controlling their body, their speech and their
mind.

|

Some do Raja Yoga: morals, concentration,
Yoga postures, breathing and meditation;
Others study Scriptures of this or that kind,
Meditate on these intently, heart and mind. [28]

Some, their Vital-Energy restrain:
Inhale, retain and exhale;
Others fast, control their desires,
Render the body – weak and frail. [29,30]

In all these Wisdom-Practices, Prince,
An 'Inner offering' is 'burnt', as though,
by a 'sacrificial flame'; They all serve to
purify one's heart, and thus — to reach
the Divine, Reality-Supreme. [30]

Without Wisdom-Practice, no joy can be found,
Not even in this material world down here;
Without it, Prince, what can one ever hope for,
In the Hereafter, or any other sphere? [31]

All these are Wisdom-Practices,
They all entail action, you see;
Remember "I am not the doer", this
Wisdom-Divine, will set you free. [32]

Without this Wisdom you mistake,
The active doer to be you;
Your action is then mere ritual,
And limited is its due.

|

All actions lead to Wisdom, Prince,
Like wild rivers gushing into calm sea;
Bit by bit they purify your heart
'Till Wisdom Divine dawns within. [33]

The meek who have Realized the Truth
Will help you this Wisdom attain;
If you but devoutly ask their help,
Humble yourself and serve them. [34]

Never again shall Ignorance deceive you,
When in your heart this Wisdom dawns and shines;
In this Wisdom's light all creation you'll see,
Within your Inner-Self, and in the Divine. [35]

Be you the foulest of sinners, this
Wisdom, past your sins, has you sweep;
Like a raft, smoothly traversing
Dark waters, no matter how deep. [36]

Wood burnt to ashes, O Prince,
Will it bear fruit, its leaves again bloom?
Likewise, one's Karma, past deed imprints,
By this fire of Wisdom are consumed. [37]

Purifier strong as Inner-Self Wisdom
World over – does not exist;
In due time, Prince, you'll find it within,
If in Yoga – you persist. [38]

Who gains Wisdom? The faithful one,
Heart devoted, senses restrained;
Once Wisdom is earned – then directly
Freedom, Peace Supreme is attained. [39]

The ignorants, faithless, doubters,
To their own destruction they steer;
How'd they enjoy any pleasure,
In the Hereafter or down here? [40]

When, through Yoga, one desire-less acts,
Doubts rent asunder in Wisdom Divine;
When the heart is stable in Inner-Self's joy,
Then one is free, by nothing confined. [41]

"But, does Inner-Self truly exist?"
Still I see that doubt in your eyes;
Slash darkness, with your Wisdom sword, Prince!
Then in Yoga of Action arise! [42]

"GITA IS A BOOK OF UNIVERSAL SELF-REALIZATION, INTRODUCING MAN TO HIS TRUE SELF, THE SOUL. IT IS THE GOLDEN PATH, BOTH FOR THE BUSY MAN OF THE WORLD AND FOR THE HIGHEST SPIRITUAL ASPIRANT."

—

Yogananda
Author of 'Autobiography of a Yogi'
Considered 'father' of Yoga in the West

PREFACE TO CHAPTER FIVE

Chapter Five explores further the relation between Action, Renunciation, and Wisdom. Tell me which is better – asks the
Prince – being active in the world, or retreating from
it, avoiding action and seeking Wisdom within? The
Gita explains that the two paths, of Action and
Wisdom, are inter-related and synergistic: acting
selflessly without desiring results cultivates Wisdom; and only when established in Wisdom can you
truly be selfless. These principles are at the very core of
Yoga. Indeed, all of the masters who have introduced yoga to
millions in the West, from Yogananda to Iyengar and others,
viewed the Gita as capturing the very essence of yoga, beyond
the physical practice. Your life is a journey – says the Gita
– from identifying with your lower, materialistic nature to
reconnecting with your higher Inner-Self. Like a lotus flower, rooted in mud yet with its white petals floating ef-
fortlessly on muddy waters, we all journey from 'mud'
to 'lotus'. From worldliness, to being in the world
but not of the world: "Desires aside, all actions
an offering — the Wise rests on action, by
action untainted; Like a pure lotus leaf
in muddy waters — resting on water remaining not wetted."

CHAPTER FIVE

Yoga of Renunciation

PRINCE:

You extol renouncing action,
Yet Action's Path you also praise;
Now tell me conclusively, Master,
Which is the better of these? [1]

MASTER:

Renouncing action, and acting,
Each, done well – will liberate;
Both are better, O Prince
Then merely refusing to act. [2]

Renunciation isn't inaction,
But giving-up 'like' and 'dislike' thoughts;
One's bonds of Illusion are shed, when
Nothing is rejected, or sought. [3]

Wisdom-Yoga, say the Ignorant,
Differs from Yoga-of-Action;
Not so – truly established in one,
Rewards of them both you obtain. [4]

The paths of Action and Wisdom
Are one – to the same goal both lead;
Wisdom seekers and men of Action,
Both meet there, equally freed. [5]

But renouncing action is difficult, Prince,
If on Action-Yoga practice you're not keen;
This Yoga purifies the meditator,
Leading one to quickly attain the Supreme. [6]

Devoted to the Action Path,
Mind pure, body, senses restrained;
Seeing one's own Inner-Self – in all,
One acts – by action not stained. [7]

"I do nothing at all" the Wise never forgets,
Heart united with the Divine, enlightened soul;
Whether grasping, moving, sleeping or breathing,
Whatever is heard, or what the eyes behold. [8]

Eyes open or shut, whatever seen or heard,
Silently, without words, the Wise always knows:
"I do not see any sight — I do not hear,
'Tis the senses that see and hear all those". [9]

Desires aside, all actions an offering,
The Wise rests on action, by action untainted;
Like a pure lotus leaf in muddy waters,
Resting on water, remaining not wetted. [10]

For Action-Yogis, unattached,
Mind, body, senses are but tools;
Actions purify their hearts, Prince,
They know "I act not", they're not fooled. [11]

Detached from fruits of one's actions,
Peace Eternal – one will have found;
Whereas one who craves actions' fruits,
By desire – is driven and bound. [12]

Happy is one who through discernment,
From one's own actions is freed;
Though dwelling in body and senses, yet
Causes not their action, does no deed. [13]

God neither acts not drives action
Nor action to fruit does He link;
'Tis Nature alone that acts, Prince,
You'll know it, if deeply you think. [14]

God is everywhere, and is ever perfect,
What has He with man's virtue or with man's
sin? Inner-Self's light, by Ignorance is veiled,
Man thus identifies with his actions' din. [15]

But when Inner-Self's light dispels Ignorance,
Then from within, this Wisdom-light shines;
Radiant sun, lighting all that surrounds us,
And all around us we behold the Divine. [16]

Intellect absorbed in the Divine,
Their very Self is the Divine;
Knowing it – they never fall back,
Goal attained, they're firm in Divine. [17]

To the Enlightened, all are equal: a Priest
Pure-minded, in one's vows steadfast;
A cow, an elephant, a mangy dog,
And a wretched dog-eater, outcast. [18]

Even here in this world, O Prince,
All's overcome by equal mind;
The Divine is taintless, equal to all,
The Wise thus abides – in the Divine. [19]

Mind stable, illusions cleared,
In the Divine – the Wise finds rest;
Not thrilled attaining the pleasant,
Nor by the unpleasant beset. [20]

Unattached to the sense world, outside,
On Inner-Self alone – intent;
The Wise meditates, retreats within,
Finds boundless joy – and is content. [21]

Like a womb that breeds but sorrow, are
Senses' contacts with sound 'n sight;
They start, O Prince, and they end,
For the Wise – they hold no delight. [22]

Whilst in this world, not yet freed from
Bonds of the body – one who can
Resist anger, fend-off desire,
Is a true Yogi – a happy man. [23]

Only the Yogi who's ever
Rejoicing, Illumined – within;
Attains absolute Freedom, and
Verily becomes the Divine. [24]

Flaws burnt, seeming Ignorance – felled,
Such Yogis gain Freedom Supreme;
Their Inner-Self – they now see in all,
Intent on the good of all beings. [25]

Happy is the true renunciate,
Freedom, Bliss Divine on all sides;
Thoughts reined, free from anger, desire,
In the Divine – one constantly abides. [26]

Senses debarred from the world external,
Gaze resting between the eyebrows;
Inhales, exhales, within the nostrils,
Controlling the breath as it flows, [27]

Free from anger, desire and fear,
Restraining senses, intellect and mind;
Freedom is the Meditator's goal,
For certain – Liberation one'll find. [28]

One who thus knows Me, Divine,
Object of all paths and prayers, O Prince;
Lord of all worlds, friend of all beings,
Most surely – attains to My Peace. [29]

"THE BHAGAVAD GITA IS ONE OF THE GREATEST
SPIRITUAL TREASURES OF HUMANITY."
—

Eckhart Tolle

PREFACE TO CHAPTER SIX

Chapter six discusses Meditation, a method of training and calming the mind, which is central to inner journey and Yoga. You begin your inner quest convinced that you are your intellect, emotions and thoughts. Meditation opens the door for you to go beyond noisy thoughts and emotions, thereby experiencing, at least in part, the blissful quietude within – your true, Divine, Inner-Self. Meditation practice is simple, but since, as the Prince observes, the mind is wilder than the wind, it is a practice that requires patient perseverance. You initially turn to Meditation, simply to give your mind a much needed rest; like the rest Yoga gives your body. Over time though, Meditation practice leads to a profound Wisdom transformation which changes your experience of the world, and your functioning in it. You begin your journey seeking happiness outside; through the alchemy of Meditation, you find it where it always was, within. As this transformation settles in, you find you no longer depend on the external world for your happiness: "Having obtained it, one now knows — this treasure's superior to all; Knowledge so certain cannot be shaken — though greatest of sorrows befall."

CHAPTER SIX

Yoga of Meditation

MASTER:

A Yogi, a true Renunciate,
Does one's Duty, fruits doesn't expect;
A monk is not a Renunciate
If one's vows cause Duty's neglect. [1]

Yoga, O Prince, do understand,
Is merely renunciation;
Fearing for future or results
Befit not Yoga of Action. [2]

For the Yoga Seeker, at first,
Action's good – it quiets the mind;
When mind is stilled, firm in Yoga,
Now it's quiescence – one would find. [3]

When attachment, even in thought,
To sense-objects and action – is gone;
One is then considered to be
In Yoga – established, enthroned. [4]

Lift yourself by your Self, O Prince,
And let not your Self flounder low;
You yourself are your only friend
As well as your very worst foe. [5]

Your divine, Inner-Self is your friend,
Mind's lower nature – your worst foe;
Bond with your pure, divine nature,
Mind, subdued – will follow in tow. [6]

One who's established in Inner-Self,
Mind serene, all cravings restrained;
Knows no disquiet, in heat or cold,
Shame or honor, pleasure or pain. [7]

When one experiences Wisdom-Divine,
Content, by sense-objects no more swayed
Divinely-United, while still in this flesh
One equally views – stone, gold or clay. [8]

Greatest is one who's even-minded
To kind friends, and vicious foes;
Righteous and rogues, haters and kin
And to them who are none of those. [9]

Let the Yogi retreat, alone, secluded,
Over body and mind let one practice control;
Shedding all hopes, shedding worldly possessions,
Constant Inner-Self meditation is one's goal. [10]

Setting one's seat, comfortable, firm,
In a place calm, quiet and clean;
Seated in a seat not too high or low,
With cloth and holy grass cushioned. [11]

Seated there, patient, one practices control
Over one's senses, emotions, and thought;
Meditating this way, mind single-pointed,
Gradually, but surely purifies one's heart. [12]

One's posture is motionless, firm,
Body, head and neck – still, upright;
Inner gaze – to the tip of the nose,
Mind steady not straying about. [13]

Mind controlled from its restless drift,
Fearless, in celibacy steadfast;
Let one sit, mind focused, serene,
Goal Supreme, Divine – reach at last. [14]

Thus, the Yogi strictly maintains
Mind balanced, controlled at all times;
Peace one attains, leading to Freedom,
Abiding in Me, the Divine. [15]

Yoga is not possible, O Prince,
For one who overeats or fasts;
Not for one who's oversleeping
Nor one who over-exerts oneself. [16]

Let one ever be moderate,
Ever steady in all one's ways;
In sleep, waking, eating and exercise,
Yoga removes all one's pains. [17]

Resting, focused – in Inner Self,
With perfect control of the mind;
Freed from any desire, 'tis said,
One's united in the Divine. [18]

Like a lamp's flame, which flickers not,
When it is in a windless place;
So is the Yogi's mind, which is
Focused, steady, on Inner-Self. [19]

When the mind, restrained by Yoga,
Within it-Self quietly rests;
'Tis then one experiences one's True Self,
Knows joyous content in one's breast. [20]

Then does such purified heart know
Bliss that's beyond what senses can;
Established in this Reality
Never to wander again. [21]

Having obtained it, one now knows
This treasure is superior to all;
Knowledge so certain cannot be shaken
Though greatest of sorrows befall. [22]

Yoga parts us from pain, O Prince,
Pain we thought would always be there;
Practice it therefore, determined,
Be joyful and never despair. [23]

Utterly abandon desires, Prince,
Know they all arise from your thought;
The wild pack of senses – restrain,
Discerning what's Real from what's not. [24]

Patiently, O Prince, bit by bit,
Let one gradually calm one's mind;
On divine Inner-Self focus inwards,
Not letting the mind wander round. [25]

Time after time – mind will stray,
Outward, by senses – drawn away;
Time and again it be withdrawn,
Focused on Inner-Self alone. [26]

Supreme Bliss one verily knows,
The Yogi whose mind is serene;
Who's become at one with the Divine,
Desires all hushed, free from sin. [27]

Free from vice, mind constantly trained,
Meditating deeply on the Divine;
Divinely touched, one's path now clear,
Thus the Yogi knows Bliss Sublime. [28]

Pure divine heart, sees but Divine,
In every creature large or small;
Knows one's Inner-Self – in all beings,
And in Inner-Self – sees all. [29]

One who sees Me, the Divine, in all, and
In Me sees all beings, every bird 'n tree;
Never am I separated from such Yogi,
Nor such Yogi – separated from Me. [30]

Established in Unity, with Me, Divine,
Worshipping Me devoutly, in all beings;
In Me, Divine, such Yogi safely abides,
Whatever be one's conduct or what life brings. [31]

Bearing each creature's joy and pain
As though they were one's very own;
Highest Yogi, sees all around
But one's own Inner Self alone. [32]

PRINCE:
Master, you describe this Yoga
As constant union with the Divine;
How can such a state be constant?
Ever so restless is the mind! [33]

Roughened by worldly desires,
Restless, unyielding is man's mind;
How shall I tame it, O Master,?
Wind itself does not seem as wild! [34]

MASTER:
Yes, Prince, mind is restless, no doubt,
Its control – is hard to maintain;
But it can be done, if you persist
And all your desires – restrain. [35]

One who reins not senses and mind
Will find this Yoga difficult;
But one self-restrained, persevering,
Using right means – will master it. [36]

PRINCE:
But what of one who strives not enough,
And though faithful – yet hasn't stayed;
One who does not reach perfection
For one's mind from Yoga has strayed? [37]

Both life paths, of spirit and matter,
Doesn't one miss by and by?
Isn't one lost, unsupported,
An orphan cloud, lost in the sky? [38]

This doubt, Master,
Has me distraught;
Only you can
Dispel this thought. [39]

MASTER:

No, my son, such seeker's not lost,
Not in this world nor in the next;
Know that one who seeks the Divine
Shall never succumb to ill fate. [40]

One who has fallen from practice
Will still get to heaven for sure;
Then, in due time, would be born again
To parents successful and pure. [41]

One may even be born, O Prince,
To wise Yogic parents to bear;
Though such birth is hard to come by
For in our world, these are rare. [42]

One would then, assimilate anew
Wisdom acquired before;
And to reach the goal of perfection,
Would then strive for even more. [43]

Through practice of previous lives
To Union-Divine path one's drawn;
Mere wishing it is loftier than
All religious rites one performs. [44]

Through many births and tireless striving
All one's shortcomings to cleanse;
This Yogi moves towards perfection
And reaches this goal in the end. [45]

Be a Yogi, Prince! A Yogi's best,
Who tirelessly seeks the Divine;
Greater than scholars and doers
Or ascetics who purge body 'n mind. [46]

One who thus faithfully merges
One's Inner Self, in Me, Divine;
Such Yogi, above all others,
I ever consider as Mine. [47]

"THIS IS THE BOOK THAT ENLIGHTENED ME
MOST IN MY WHOLE LIFE."
—

Johann Wolfgang Göethe

PART TWO

Path of Devotion

PREFACE TO CHAPTER SEVEN

Chapter seven introduces us to Gita's dazzlingly poetic second path, the Path of Devotion. From a focus on Action and on how to act wisely in the world, we now move on to the realm of poetic intuition, and of cultivating our emotional intelligence and Devotion. It introduces us to an inner journey that is not attainable through efforts, or technique or intellectualization – but through poetic simplicity and intuitive ecstasy. It is the Divine itself, inviting us to peek through the 'veil' of Nature, and experience its underlying serene glory: "I am the sweet fragrance of earth — as well as the brilliance of fire; Know me, O Prince, seed eternal — all that grows and blossoms I sire." Remember that 'the Divine' speaking here is not some external, boastful 'god'. Rather, it is the inner voice of your own soul, calling you from within. Calling you to awaken and realize that you are Life itself, not this fragile, mortal body and mind. Inviting you to experience the sublime harmony in Nature outside, and then learn to similarly recognize this Divine unity within, as who you truly are: "Penance of the ascetics, am I — Life itself in all that's alive; Intellect of the intelligent — and in the active their drive."

CHAPTER SEVEN

Wisdom and Realization

MASTER:

Hear now, O Prince, how to surely, fully,
Know Me – the Divine;
Practicing the Yoga I taught you,
Devoted to Me, heart and mind. [1]

Scripture's knowledge – I'll teach you
And its Realization as well;
When one has attained to these, Prince,
There's nothing more to know or to tell. [2]

Who bothers to seek this ultimate Freedom?
One amongst thousands of women and men;
How many reach it, of all Freedom seekers?
Of thousands of seekers, perhaps one will attain. [3]

There are eight components to Nature, O Prince,
Which itself, remember, is but the Divine:
Five elements – Earth, Water, Fire, Air and Space –
And three that rule them – Ego, Intellect, Mind. [4]

Consciousness is Nature's higher essence,
behind Nature, unknown, It inscrutably
reigns; It is the source of all that's alive,
Prince – the entire universe it sustains. [5]

Recognize Nature and Consciousness,
As two wombs of all: sentient, inanimate;
I, the Divine, am the source of them both,
Universe's seed, from which they all emanate. [6]

Causeless cause of all causes, O Prince,
That I am – Essence-Divine;
Know that all worlds, and all beings,
Like threaded pearls, on Me are strung. [7]

Sun and moon – I am their light,
Essence of water – in sea and rain;
God's essence – 'Om' sound, and silence,
And in man – I am the humane. [8]

I am the sweet fragrance of earth,
As well as the brilliance of fire;
Know me, O Prince, seed eternal,
All that grows and blossoms – I sire. [9]

Penance of ascetics, am I,
Life itself – in all that's alive;
Intellect of the intelligent,
And in the active – their drive. [10]

Mightiness of the strong – I am,
Unattached, desiring none;
In all beings – I am life's passion,
Natural and in moderation. [11]

I am source Divine of Nature's three Facets,
They are within Me, though I'm not part of them;
From these three – Purity, Activeness, Dullness –
All that is alive and insentient stems. [12]

Nature's-Facets' dance – in and 'round us,
Fools the whole world – that's all it sees;
Therefore the world discerns Me not,
Unchanging and separate from these. [13]

This is Nature's-Veil's Illusion,
It's Nature-Facets veil the Divine;
One who in Me, Divine, takes refuge,
Sees through it – Me one will find. [14]

Evildoers, trapped by Nature's-Veil,
Lowest of men, they seek not the Divine;
Thinking "I am the body" they worship it,
See it as all, and thus cause but harm. [15]

Of those purged by their righteousness,
Four types turn to Me, the Divine:
The Knowledge-seeker, the Distressed,
Joy-seeker, and the Discerning-one. [16]

Of these, the Discerning-one is highest,
Devoted, and in Me, united and near;
So dear am I, the Divine, to such soul, and
It, to My heart – is special and dear. [17]

Surely these four are all noble, O Prince,
But the Discerning-one is My very own;
I, Divine, am the only goal for such soul,
Whose mind is ever fixed on Me alone. [18]

Through innumerable life-cycles,
Bit by bit, one's mind thus evolves;
Knowing – all this is but the Divine,
How rare is such a great soul. [19]

Those whose discrimination
By worldly desires has dulled;
Pray to one god or another,
Craving for worldly rewards. [20]

Whatever god one thus turns to,
Faithfully praying and sincere;
I, the Divine, strengthen that faith,
Making it firm without fear. [21]

One then prays to one's chosen god,
Newly firmed faith by one's side;
One's prayers are answered – although
In truth, 'tis I alone who Provide. [22]

But praying for transient fruits
Is of paltry value, you see;
Those worshipping gods – gods attain,
Revere Me, Divine – you reach Me. [23]

The Ignorant think that I, bodiless,
Am now mortal, man I've become;
They know not My nature, unchanging,
I Am the Divine – I am One. [24]

By Nature's-Veil, O Prince,
From the masses – I am hidden;
This deluded world knows Me not,
I, who am birthless, unchanging. [25]

All creation's beings I know,
In past, at present and future;
But none of these beings, O Prince,
Truly knows – My unborn nature. [26]

From birth, all beings are deluded
In thinking that this world is real;
This Illusion, O Prince, stems from
The 'likes' and 'dislikes' that they feel. [27]

Gradually, hearts of the righteous
Are purified by their good deeds;
The Divine is their only goal,
From illusory-opposites they're freed. [28]

Those taking refuge in Me, Divine,
From death, old age – seek to be free;
They fully Realize the Divine
In all deeds and all that they see. [29]

In Spirit, Matter, and Action,
Those who thus know Me, the Divine;
Even at death – in Me they're merged,
Firm in faith and focus of mind. [30]

"QUANTUM THEORY WILL NOT LOOK
RIDICULOUS TO PEOPLE WHO HAVE READ
VEDANTA"
—
Werner Karl Heisenberg

"MULTIPLICITY IS ONLY APPARENT. THE UNITY
AND CONTINUITY OF WAVE MECHANICS IS
ENTIRELY CONSISTENT WITH THE VEDANTA
CONCEPT OF ALL IN ONE."
—
Erwin Schrödinger

"I GO INTO THE UPANISHADS TO ASK
QUESTIONS."
—
Niels Bohr

PREFACE TO CHAPTER EIGHT

Chapter eight dives into a deeper discourse on the nature of
the unchanging Reality, which underlies the ever-changing
phenomenal-world around us, and provides guidance
on how to experience it. It is surprising to find that
Gita's poetic verses are admired not only by poets and spiritual seekers, but also by some of the
brightest physicists of all times. Versed in Yoga's
Vedanta philosophy, which the Gita presents, they
assert its alignment with Quantum theory. The world we
experience through our senses and intellect – says the Gita
– does not exist as solidly as it appears. The multitude of
separate objects we experience, are part of an underlying
Unity. And that underlying Unity, that Consciousness, that
Divine – is who we really are. Everything in your dream
last night, is made out of ...dream! Right? The 'you' fig-
ure in the dream, and the mountain you climbed. They
seemed separate, but in truth they are part of a Unity, are both 'made of dream'. We think our current waking state is different, but it really isn't:
"All's within it and it 'fills' all — this supreme, Reality Divine; You gain Wisdom, Know it directly — by total
devotion, heart and mind."

CHAPTER EIGHT

Path to the Divine

PRINCE:

What are Inner-Self and Divine, O Master,
Can you please explain?
What's the Material Plane you spoke of,
And what is the Spiritual Plane? [1]

What is God, to whom we all pray,
Who governs the Action Plane? And
At death, how are You revealed to those
Whose senses and mind are reined? [2]

MASTER:

The Divine is the Reality,
Ever unchanged, undying;
Inner-Self – is but a name for it,
Inner essence of every being. [3]

The Material Plane is Nature,
Perishable, ever in change;
Spiritual Plane – 'fills' it all,
Spirit in nature, soul in man.

|

I alone, Divine, inhabit this body, Prince,
I am Consciousness, all actions I rule;
Spirit and Matter are of Me and in Me,
To Me all pray, their refuge, their jewel. [4]

At death, when leaving the body,
On Me let one focus the mind;
Know this for certain, O Prince,
Thus one merges with Me, the Divine. [5]

Departing this body you reach
That which you remember at last;
Your mind is filled with this thought, for
You've thought of it much in the past. [6]

Therefore, ever remember Me
And your natural Duty – carry-out;
Heart and mind ever on Me, Divine,
Thus reach Me you will – no doubt. [7]

Meditate regularly, Prince,
Constant practice steadies your mind;
Let not your mind stray and wander,
Thus, in time, you'll reach the Divine. [8]

Omniscient God, primordial ruler of all,
Beyond Ignorance' dark, radiant as sun;
Inconceivable, minuter than minute,
On Him one should meditate at all times. [9]

For then, as one leaves the body,
Heart devoted and mind steadfast;
Life-breath fixed between the eyebrows,
To that Supreme God – one departs. [10]

About the Immortal, O Prince,
Let me now instruct you in brief;
Renunciates enter into It,
Reigning over desire and grief. [11]

At death, when one leaves the body,
Let one shut all the senses' gates;
Focusing the mind at the heart,
Life-force raised to crown of the head. [12]

Uttering Om, Divine's essence,
And focusing on it in thought;
When thus leaving the body
One reaches the Divine, and strays not. [13]

The Yogi meditates daily, for years,
From thought-Divine never apart;
Easily attains Me, Divine,
For we're ever united at heart. [14]

Great souls that find Me, the Divine,
Freedom supreme – verily find;
They are not re-born here again,
In this world of impermanence 'n pain. [15]

Recurring death and rebirth, O Prince,
Bind all worlds, even gods' throne;
But one who reaches Me, Divine,
Shall never again be re-born. [16]

In truth, it is but consciousness,
This world, which so real would seem;
It is much like a dream world,
In which all is made out of dream.
|
A Cosmic Day is therefore described
As well as a Cosmic Night;
Cosmic Day – a thousand eons long,
A thousand – the Cosmic Night. [17]

Cosmic Day dawns, all creation emerges,
As if God began dreaming this vast 'cosmic-dream';
Then back to its source all creation dissolves,
As this 'dream' ends and Cosmic Night falls. [18]

From their unseen essence they all appear,
Dissolving back to it, helpless, time and again;
Their action, born of desire and Ignorance,
'Tis that, Prince, which binds all creatures, all men.
|
Likewise, with every thought you think,
First 'you' then 'the world' are feigned;
And in each gap between thoughts
Both these notions dissolve yet again. [19]

But know that behind all this,
The seen world and its source unseen;
There is Reality, O Prince,
Eternal, ever unchanging. [20]

That is the highest goal, Prince,
This Reality, Absolute Truth;
Those reaching it – are forever free
From endless Death and Rebirth. [21]

All's within It, and It 'fills' all,
This supreme, Reality Divine;
You gain Wisdom, Know it directly,
By total devotion – heart and mind.
|
With the same direct certitude
You now 'know': "I am a man";
By Lord's Grace you'll wake up to Realize:
"Divine Reality – I Am". [22]

Now let me declare to you two paths, Prince,
When leaving the body let one choose one's way:
The Path of Light, leading to the Divine,
Or Dark Path, to endless Rebirth and Decay. [23]

Path of Light leads to the Divine,
Free from Death and Rebirth on end;
Established in Wisdom Divine,
One is never reborn again. [24]

The Dark Path leads to heaven first,
Then back to human birth again;
Path of those who heed moral decrees,
Yet still crave the fruits that these gain. [25]

Light Path and Dark Path, primordial,
The one – Liberation attains;
The other – a brief taste of heaven
And then – shackled life back again. [26]

Comprehending these two paths, Prince,
No Yogi – will ever sway;
Be steadfast therefore in Yoga!
And from Path of Light do not stray. [27]

Moral decrees do bear good fruits,
This is true, as all Scriptures teach;
But a Yogi craves no fruits at all,
The highest, Divine, one will reach. [28]

PREFACE TO CHAPTER NINE

Chapter nine beautifully describes the 'royal science' of Mys-
ticism, or non-intellectual knowledge. Intellect cannot grasp
Reality – says the Gita – just as eyes cannot see sounds.
How do you know you are man and not tomato?
How does an actor know he's not really King Lear?
Could you, or the actor, be convinced otherwise
by intellectual debate? You know through non-intellectual, experiential knowledge. It is a Knowing that
is like opening the door to let sunlight in. You cannot fight
the darkness of Ignorance. You merely open the door to let-
in the ever abundant light of Wisdom. Wisdom, like sunlight,
is a curious thing. It is not something you 'get' or can 'keep'
to yourself, nor is it even something you can 'give' someone
(or withhold from another). As you open the gates of your
heart, you find yourself humbled by Grace, showered by
Light that's clearly not yours. All you can do, and do
so gladly, is accept Gita's inclusive, non-sectarian invitation, to cleanse the 'mirror' of your heart, so
that it reflects this Light freely onto others:
"Like sun, I shine onto all beings — could I
shine onto anyone more? But My devotees reflect My light — for they
have opened heart's door."

Yoga of Mysticism

MASTER:
Secret of secrets – hear now, O Prince,
Who's free from fault-finding and envy;
Wisdom Supreme, direct, not cognitive,
Know it – and forever be free. [1]

Royal science, kingly secret,
Imperishable – once gained;
Intuitive, fit for the Mystic,
Best purifier – its practice is plain. [2]

Those lacking faith in this Wisdom,
Me, the Divine – they cannot attain;
Back they must all return, O Prince,
To mortals' path – of death and pain. [3]

I, Divine, fill this universe,
My abstract form – eyes cannot see;
Though I'm not inside any creature,
All creatures exist within Me. [4]

They aren't physically in Me,
I am their essence, from It they flow;
This is My divine mystery,
Its nature – strive earnestly to know. [5]

Blowing winds, rest always in space,
Though they touch it not, you see;
Likewise, all migrant beings touch Me not,
And yet – ever rest within Me. [6]

All beings arise from Me, Divine,
In Me they dissolve and they wend; As
Dream-figures arise in a dreamer's mind
And set – when the dream ends. [7]

I, Divine, master of Nature,
Which itself drives all living things;
Time and again, unending, helpless,
All creatures I send forth from My Being. [8]

I'm not bound by these actions,
Creating this world, dissolving it, Prince;
For I'm indifferent to their fruits,
In truth, I am but a Witness. [9]

Just as sun gives life to all,
Serene witness – devoid of intent;
I, Divine, vitalize Nature,
All that's alive or insentient. [10]

Fools pass blindly by My abode,
Clad in this, my human form, frail;
I am Lord Supreme of all beings,
Yet, grasp my Divine Nature – they fail. [11]

Vain are their hopes and actions,
Intellect clouded, knowledge in vain;
God-less, they worship body alone,
To their Lower Nature – gave in. [12]

But the great souls seek refuge, O Prince,
In Me alone, the Divine;
Immortal source of all living beings,
On Me – they focus their mind, [13]

Devout, they aspire to Me,
To moral ways – strictly adhere;
Venerating Me, the Divine,
To Me they pray, Me they revere. [14]

Others follow the Wisdom Path,
Within, without – see but Divine;
Some worship Me as a deity, external, or
As numerous gods, all aspects of Mine. [15]

I am all Mantras and rituals
Taught by all Scriptures divine;
Prayer words and act of praying
Are all but aspects of Mine. [16]

World's mother and father – I am,
Dispenser of all actions' fruit;
I Am the One, the sacred sound Om,
All Scriptures and Wisdom Absolute. [17]

The Witness and the Goal – I am,
This world I create and uphold;
I am its seed and dissolution,
The Refuge, the Friend, the Abode. [18]

The heat of the sun I am, Prince,
The rain – I send forth and I pause;
I'm death and immortality,
The manifest world and its cause. [19]

Those missing Scriptures' deep meaning
Heed religion's decrees and rites;
The heaven they craved they do reach,
And take joy in heaven's delights. [20]

These heavenly pleasures they briefly enjoy,
Then, merit exhausted they must take rebirth;
Righteous in conduct, yet still craving reward,
They're trapped in this cycle of Heaven and Earth. [21]

But those who ever meditate Me alone,
The Divine-in-all, inseparable from them;
Devoted, they know not desire nor fear,
Their needs I provide, their possessions defend. [22]

Even those praying faithfully,
To this or that god – are devout;
To Me, Divine, they are turning,
Though misguided and roundabout. [23]

For all prayers are prayed onto Me,
In truth, I, the Divine, alone Am;
Those praying to gods, knowing Me not,
Must be reborn – time and again. [24]

Pray to a god and you'll reach it, Prince,
Invoke spirits – you reach their plane;
Entreat nature's powers – them you get to,
Devoted to Me – Me, Divine you attain. [25]

Whatever one may offer Me,
A leaf, a flower, some water or fruit;
I, the Divine, accept their love,
When offered pure-hearted, devout. [26]

All your actions and prayers, Prince,
All you eat, or give or think of;
Your Wisdom-Practices too,
Let them all be an offering of love. [27]

Thus you're freed from your Action Bonds,
A net of good and bad fruits – these cast;
Focused on Me, renouncing these fruits,
Free, you will reach Me at last. [28]

Like Sun, I shine onto all beings,
Could I shine onto anyone more?
But My devotees reflect My light
For they have opened heart's door. [29]

Though one may be tainted, O Prince,
By life-long wrongdoing and fault;
Saintly one is, if rightly resolved,
To Me, the Divine – devout. [30]

Holiness soon reforms one's nature,
Peace eternal one thus surely finds;
Know certain – one does not perish,
Who's devoted to Me, the Divine. [31]

My door is open to all, Prince,
Lowest of low, vilest of men;
Taking devout refuge in Me,
Me, Divine – one surely attains. [32]

How much easier is the way, then,
For those of a fortunate birth?
Seek joy in Me, not in the world,
Life is short, O Prince, time is dearth. [33]

On Me fix your mind, to Me be devoted,
See Me, the Divine – in all that you see;
Your ego subdued, in Me find your refuge,
Offer all actions – as prayer onto Me.
|
With Me – thus uniting yourself,
In your quest, O Prince, to be Free;
Me, the Divine – your Goal Supreme,
Most surely, you'll come onto Me. [34]

PREFACE TO CHAPTER TEN

Chapter ten, one of Gita's most poetic chapters, provides a
dazzling sampling of Divine Reality's glorious manifestations,
in the world around us, as well as within. In our 'forgetfulness', we experience ourselves as petty body-mind
creatures. Separated from, and in conflict with,
each other, and the world around us. The Gita reminds us we are all 'waves' in one indivisible 'ocean';
in truth we are 'ocean' itself. Internally, we mistakenly
identify with qualities of our mind and personality. These
too, the Gita reminds us, are only 'internal waves' of that same
indivisible 'ocean'. In our confusion, we often seek to retreat
from the world outside, in order to 'find spirituality'. Perhaps
this religion, or technique, is better? Perhaps that teacher or
teaching will bring me joy? Such confusion arises in us. Gita's
tenth chapter acts like a magical balm. Rather than retreat
from the world, it follows your gaze as you survey it,
outside and within, softly echoing in your heart: all
this is Spirit, is Divine. The chapter concludes, after
all this cataloguing, poetically asking: "But tell
me, O Prince, what need you know — all
of these details so fine? Suffice it you
know I Exist — the whole world
upheld by a fragment of Mine"

CHAPTER TEN

Divine Glory

MASTER:

Once again, hear this, my dear Prince,
Wisdom supreme – my highest word;
I know you delight in hearing it,
And teach you, for your soul's good. [1]

My beginning and source – none knows,
Not highest of sages nor gods;
For in every manner and way,
I am their quintessence and source. [2]

Only that soul who Knows Me, Divine,
As the Lord of all worlds, unborn;
Is free from sin, free from delusion,
Such soul of all mortals alone. [3]

All human diversified facets and traits:
Intellect, wisdom, non-delusion, restraint,
Pleasure 'n pain, suffering 'n joy, birth as well
as death — truth, calm, forbearance, fear and
fearlessness, [4]

Harming no creature, equal vision to all,
Misfortune and hardship, distinction and fame;
Contentment and charity, senses controlled,
From Me, the Divine, all these qualities came. [5]

The Five Elements the world is made of
Arise from Me, the Divine;
As do man's facets, which are intellect,
Sub-consciousness, ego and mind. [6]

One who truly knows Me, Divine,
In all of these manifold form;
Of this there is no doubt, O Prince,
In my Yoga – one then becomes firm. [7]

I, Divine, am the essence and source of all,
As water is essence of all ocean's waves;
The Wise directly experience this Wisdom,
And thus are united in Me while alive. [8]

They live wholly absorbed in Me,
On Me they have focused their mind;
Enlightening each other they live,
Delighted in Me, the Divine. [9]

Those wholly devoted to Me,
With love and full dedication;
Soon indeed reach Me, the Divine,
Through my grace of discrimination. [10]

One who's focused on Me, Divine,
The Inner-Self of one's own heart;
My shining lamp of Self-Knowledge,
Dispels one's Ignorance' dark. [11]

PRINCE:

You are indeed the Divine,
The Light, Reality Supreme;
Eternal, birthless, Lord of Lords;
Abiding in hearts of all beings. [12]

Sages of yore,
Your praises sing;
Now to mine ears,
Your lips reaffirm. [13]

My Master, Lord – I believe you,
Holy truth is your every word;
Even gods – your glory know not,
Origin and Light of the world. [14]

You are the world's very essence,
In every being – their Inner-Self;
You yourself alone know, my Lord,
Your Self – by yourself. [15]

Teach me then, my Master, my Lord,
I implore you, pray save no words;
Your forms which fill all creation,
Pray tell me them all – if you would. [16]

Tell me, revered Master and Lord:
Meditating constant on thee,
Under which guises and what shapes,
Your Oneness I must learn to see. [17]

Tell me again, I tire not,
List your forms and powers divine;
In your every word, O Master,
Nectar immortal – I find. [18]

MASTER:
Very well, I'll teach you my forms,
But only the main ones – I'll name;
For their variants and details, Prince,
Are unnumbered and without end. [19]

I am the Inner-Self, O Prince,
In each and every mortal's heart;
Of all creation's beings – I am
Their end, their present and their start. [20]

I am all gods and deities,
In all their numerous names;
Of luminaries – I am sun,
Of heavens stars – the moon I am. [21]

I am all holy Scriptures,
Venerated throughout all times;
Consciousness – in living beings,
Of sense faculties – I am the mind. [22]

I am the holiest mountain,
And the quintessence of fire;
Master I am of all treasures,
Those imagined or desired. [23]

I am the bravest of victors,
And the holiest of all priests;
The vastest ocean – I am too,
Among all the lakes and the seas. [24]

I am the greatest of prophets,
Of all words – the sacred sound Om;
Of the things that cannot be moved,
The vast Himalayas – I am. [25]

All sages and saints
Of yore – I am;
Royal of beasts,
King amongst men. [26,27]

I am the sire of children,
The compassionate god of love;
Death I am too, dealing actions' fruits,
To those deserving thereof. [28,29]

Of the measurables – I am time,
Which no one can halt or delay;
Lion among all beasts – I am,
Eagle among all birds of prey. [30]

Of purifiers
Wind – I am;
Holy Ganges,
Of rivers grand. [31]

I am logic of logicians,
Creation's – start, middle and end;
Of sciences I'm Wisdom, Self-Knowledge,
The highest – one can attain. [32]

Verily I am time itself,
Dispenser of all actions' fruit;
Of all letters – I am A,
My face in all, gross and minute. [33]

I am the all devouring death,
Prosperity I am – of the rich;
Fame, firmness, forgiveness – I am,
Memory, brilliance 'n charming speech. [34]

Of seasons – I'm season of bloom,
Clever-man's luck, might of the strong;
I'm goodness of the goodhearted,
And meter and rhythm of song. [35,36]

The greatest of all poets – I am,
Of victors – I'm diplomacy;
Knowledge I am – of the learned,
Silence – of secrets' secrecy. [37,38]

I am the divine seed, O Prince,
Of anything that is alive;
No life or lifeless in this world,
Without My support can survive. [39]

My divine manifestations
Are innumerable, O Prince;
Those I have described to you here,
Are but a scant sample of these. [40]

All that is glorious in this world,
Mighty, wondrous, splendid of sight;
Know that all these emanate from
A trifling morsel of my might. [41]

But tell Me, O Prince,
Why need you know
All of these details, so fine?
Suffice it you Know – I Exist,
The whole world upheld by
A fragment of Mine. [42]

"THE BHAGAVAD GITA IS THE MOST
BEAUTIFUL PHILOSOPHICAL SONG EXISTING
IN ANY KNOWN TONGUE."
—

Robert Oppenheimer
'Father' of the Atomic bomb

Chapter eleven describes the Prince's striking mystical experience. He's heard the discourse of the previous chapter, of the
manifold manifestations of the Divine. He believes it,
but is not content with mere believing. He wants to
<u>know</u>, he wants to experience it directly: "You are
as you described yourself, I doubt it not My Lord
Supreme; And yet, your all-pervading form, with
my own eyes I wish to see." His wish is granted, and he
experiences an overwhelming 'mystic-vision', whereby the
entire universe, with all its diversity, merges into its underlying
oneness of the transcendental Divine. It is a vision so frightful-
ly imposing that "a thousand suns blazing at once, pale compared to its splendor." Robert Oppenheimer famously quoted
from this chapter, "Now I am become death, the destroyer of worlds", when seeing the blinding flash of the first
Atomic detonation. Like Oppenheimer, a pacifist charged
with building the nuclear bomb, life often places you
in 'impossible' situations. Following his example,
the Gita empowers you to carefully discern,
and responsibly embrace your life's Calling,
letting life 'enact-itself' through you:
"You are but a tool in my hand —
as in your's your pliant bow."

CHAPTER ELEVEN

Vision of the Ever-present Lord

PRINCE:

You've gracefully taught me, Master,
The truth of Divine Inner-Self;
Your words – sublime and mystical,
My Ignorance' darkness – dispelled. [1]

The source and end of all creatures,
I have learned from You in detail;
From You, whose eyes – lotus flowers,
And your untold greatness as well. [2]

You are as you described yourself,
I doubt it not, my Lord Supreme;
And yet, Your all-pervading form
With my own eyes – I wish to see. [3]

Show me, O greatest of Yogis,
If I'm worthy of such vision;
Your universal Inner-Self,
Dwelling within all, unchanging. [4]

MASTER:
Behold my manifestations,
Innumerable in shape and form;
See angels and celestial beings,
Wonders no man has seen before. [5,6]

Behold, Prince, the whole universe,
United in oneness with Me;
Life and lifeless alike, behold;
And anything else you would see. [7]

But your limited human eyes,
All this – simply cannot perceive,
I grant you divine vision, Prince,
This is my power – observe! [8]

Uttering these words to the Prince — the Master revealed His form-divine; wondrous, all-encompassing — beyond grasp of senses and mind. Speaking through countless mouths — observing through eyes without number; a thousand suns blazing at once — pale, compared to Its splendor.

And lo, at once the Prince beheld — the universe vast with its endless detail; emanate as the One — Lord of all Lords, Transcendental, Divine. Humbled, he bowed his head low — awestruck, hairs standing on end; and palms joined in prayer he addressed — the Master, the Lord once again:

PRINCE:

O, my Lord, within You I see,
Vast host of all celestial beings;
All gods, different in name and form,
Saints and angels and seraphim. [15]

Boundless, eternal – I see You,
Your vastness – who'd comprehend?
I see You, my Lord, and can find
No beginning, middle or end. [16]

Shining in every direction,
Resplendent like a thousand suns;
An ever blazing inferno,
Immeasurable, perceived by none. [17]

You are the imperishable,
Universe's treasure supreme;
World's refuge and abode – You are,
Soul of all life, immortal being. [18]

Beginning-less and without end,
No measure is there to Your might;
Your eyes – radiant sun and moon,
The whole world is lit by Your light. [19]

Pervading far reaches of earth,
And spanning the heavens above;
Beholding this, Your cosmic form,
The three worlds – shudder thereof. [20]

In You, my Lord, all gods unite,
"Thy will be done" – they all pray;
All sages, prophets and saints alike,
Worshipping and singing your praise. [21,22]

Your sight, terrible to behold,
In your manifold forms – I see;
All the worlds and I too, my Lord,
Fearfully tremble before Thee. [23,24]

Who are You, my Lord? Pray tell me,
Pray have mercy, O Lord Supreme;
From mine eyes – Your ways are hidden,
I yearn so, Your glory to see. [31]

MASTER:
I am Time, the great destroyer,
Slaying people when their time comes;
Slain – are all your battle-foes, Prince,
Without you – their life-play is done. [32]

You are but a tool in My hand,
As in yours – your pliant bow;
Knowing this – strike, seemingly kill,
Win victory over your foes. [33]

You but smite those already dead,
Their death caused by their actions past;
Stand firm and fight, O Prince – fear not!
No blame do your actions cast. [34]

The Prince bowed his head down low — as he heard these
Master's words spoken; and trembling in fear, palms
joined in prayer — turned to the Master, voice broken:

PRINCE:
It is well the world rejoices,
Takes pleasure in revering Thee;
Sages and saints before you bow,
From You, my Lord, all demons flee. [36]

Immortal, world's refuge and source,
The cause of causes, Lord supreme;
You are what is and what is-not,
And That – beyond even these. [37]

Essence, Soul and Dweller-in-all,
You are the Knower, and the Known;
In You all creation exists,
And in You – dissolves back again. [38]

To You, my Lord, I bow my head,
Lord of creation – foul and fair;
Praise, praise onto thee, my Lord,
God of all gods, a thousand prayers. [39]

No limit to Your powers, Lord,
Take our blessings – from all around;
Magnificent, You're all there is,
For everywhere 'tis You we find. [40]

By love blinded, naive, unaware,
I erred, thinking You 'Master' and 'friend';
Saw you as mortal, like myself,
Immortal Lord – I took for mere man. [41]

Oft I jested, while together
We took food, or rested, or strolled;
Have my words offended Thee, Lord?
Forgive me for being so bold. [42]

Creator of lifeless and life,
You alone are worthy of prayer;
Where in the three worlds, my Lord,
Is there anyone who would compare? [43]

Therefore, before You I humbly bow down, Lord,
I beg Your forgiveness for all my mistakes;
Forgive me as one forgives his beloved,
As father would son, a friend would his mate. [44]

Deep is my joy, fright greater still,
No man ever saw what I've seen;
Mercy, Lord, spare me this vision,
Your human form – show me again. [45,46]

MASTER:
Your vision of My cosmic form,
My mystic powers of Yoga – bore;
Magnificent and infinite,
Witnessed by no man before. [47]

Worship, rites and Scripture-study,
Austerities, and alms, O Prince;
Do not unveil My cosmic form,
Of mortals, but you – to none else. [48]

Now fear not, nor be bewildered,
Seeing this, my terrible form;
Cheer up, be brave, see here I am,
I donned My familiar form again. [49]

Speaking thus, the Master assumed — His pleasant
human form once more; consoling the Prince, dispelling
his fright — his peace once again restored.

PRINCE:

O revered Master, now I see
Your gentle human form again;
Pleasing for my eyes to behold,
I'm now composed, my nature sane. [51]

MASTER:

This form of Mine you've seen, O Prince,
Is indeed most difficult to grasp;
Even the gods up in heavens,
Are longing to see it at last. [52]

Not charity, nor rituals,
High philosophy nor penance;
None of these unveils Me, Divine,
As you, O Prince – have witnessed. [53]

But through undivided devotion,
Constantly fixed on Me, Divine;
One perceives My celestial form,
And merges into this form of Mine. [54]

One who performs all actions
As prayer and offering to Me;
Unattached, to no creature hostile,
Me, Divine, Prince – one surely will see. [55]

Chapter twelve, concludes Gita's path-of-Devotion section, and is a song-of-glory to Devotion. Which is best, asks the Prince, Devotion or Wisdom? Cultivating Devotion, or striving to intimately know the absolute Reality? Both are good – says the Gita – but Devotion is indispensable: striving for the absolute Reality is difficult, and Devotion is initially more accessible.
If you're walking in a dark alley, spooked by shadows you take to be real – pondering their nonexistence may be more difficult than taking-up means to muster courage. In its simple, loving, pragmatic voice, the Gita prescribes simple strategies, to help you out of your 'dark': Try to do this, if it's too difficult then do that, if you fail at that too – don't worry, this other will surely work. The path of Devotion is inter-woven with the paths of Action and Wisdom: It overcomes ego, hence builds on, and leads to selfless Action; and it similarly leads to and is fed by growing inner Wisdom.
The chapter's final verses, give an inspiring, poetic description of what a person of Devotion is like:
"One's home is nowhere and everywhere
— equally values praise and jeer; Silent,
mind checked, ever content —
such devotee I hold most dear."

CHAPTER TWELVE

Yoga of Devotion

PRINCE:

Some worship the Abstract God,
Some – in God-devotion are immersed;
Followers of which of these paths,
In Yoga – is better versed? [1]

MASTER:

Those whose devotion is focused,
Ceaselessly on Me, the Divine;
Their faith – steadfast and unshaken
These are the best Yogis, I find. [2]

Those worshipping the abstract God,
Omnipresent, omniscient, unchangeable;
Beyond the grasp of thought and senses,
Eternal, transcendental, indefinable, [3]

Having restrained all their senses,
Always maintaining even-mind;
Intent on welfare of all beings,
Verily they too – reach Me, Divine. [4]

But worshipping the Abstract God,
Is indeed a more difficult quest;
The soul, thinking it's a body,
Struggles to grasp – the unmanifest. [5]

Those who with devotion steadfast,
Meditate on Me, the Divine;
Dedicating all actions to Me
And in Me – their Goal Supreme find, [6]

Quickly I come to rescue those
Who are thus mind-united with Me;
From cyclic Birth-and-Death, O Prince,
Samsara's seemingly endless sea. [7]

Make me, the Divine – your goal,
On Me fix your mind, your every thought;
Thus, now and in the hereafter,
In Me, you'll reside – no doubt. [8]

If your mind cannot be constantly
Centered on Me, the Divine;
Then try on Me to re-focus,
Repeatedly, time after time. [9]

If you're unable to do so,
Dedicate all your actions to Me;
Devote your work to the Divine,
This too, Prince, will set you free. [10]

If even that you cannot do,
Yet desires still drive you to deeds;
Then renounce all fruits of your actions,
While practicing restraint of your needs. [11]

Cognition is better than mere ritual,
Meditative Wisdom – better yet;
But renouncing actions' fruits
Attains instant peace – hence it is best. [12]

One who's forgiving, hates no creature,
Friendly to all, compassionate;
Calmly accepts pleasure and pain,
Free from ego and attachment, [13]

Ever content and self-controlled,
Intellect, mind – devoted to Me;
Steadfast in meditation,
I hold dear – such devotee. [14]

Disturbs not the world, nor by it disturbed,
Free from joy, rage, envy and fear;
Devoted to Me, the Divine,
Such devotee – I hold dear. [15]

Swift, yet initiates no vain action,
Pure in body 'n thought, unbiased 'n bold;
I hold dear – such devotee,
By nothing disturbed, ready for all. [16]

Rejoices not nor saddened by,
Objects pleasant or unpleasing;
I hold dear – such devotee,
Who's craving not – nor grieving. [17]

Even-minded to heat and cold,
Pain and pleasure, honor and shame;
I hold dear – such devotee,
Who regards friend and foe – the same. [18]

One's home is nowhere and everywhere,
Equally values praise and jeer;
Silent, mind checked, ever content,
Such devotee – I hold most dear. [19]

Those faithful, practicing these Teachings,
Wisdom and Immortality – verily find;
My dearest are such devotees,
Whose goal supreme – is Me, Divine. [20]

"I OWED A MAGNIFICENT DAY TO THE GITA.
IT WAS THE FIRST OF BOOKS; IT WAS AS IF AN
EMPIRE SPOKE TO US, NOTHING SMALL OR
UNWORTHY, BUT LARGE, SERENE, CONSISTENT,
THE VOICE OF AN OLD INTELLIGENCE, WHICH
IN ANOTHER AGE AND CLIMATE HAD PONDERED
AND THUS DISPOSED OF THE SAME QUESTIONS
WHICH EXERCISE US."
—

Ralph Waldo Emerson

PART THREE

Path of Wisdom

Chapter thirteen, one of Gita's most profound discourses, opens
Gita's third path, the highest Path of Wisdom. This chapter,
and path, deal with a seemingly simple question, which
is at the very heart of our inner journey: Who Am I?
This is your life's most important question, says
the Gita, guiding you as you carefully investi-
gate. No book-knowledge can help you here. It is
a deeper knowing, a conviction, that must arise from
within. You are not this body, which is constantly changing,
aging. Nor are you this mind or this personality. These are
merely collections of memories, thoughts and emotions you
cling to and carry with you. So who am I then? Who is it that
is seeing the world through my eyes? What you are looking
for – says the Gita – is That which is looking. You are the
ever-present Witnessing awareness, the Consciousness,
the Divine. In our Ignorance, we're like an actor who's
so absorbed in the play, he forgot he's not really King
Lear. Gita invites you to turn your 'gaze' inward,
and thereby awaken to your true Divine, identity: "So near and far away is That — within, without all life all things; So subtle
it is unknowable — to the Wise
– the core of one's being."

The Field and Its Knower

PRINCE:

What is Reality, Master,
Its facets – Spirit and Matter?
What is Wisdom? What's to be Realized?
What are the Field and its Knower? [0]

MASTER:

Body and mind are called the Field, Prince,
For here one sows actions and reaps their fruits;
Knower-of-the Field is That which Witnesses
The body and mind, and all their pursuits. [1]

Know Me, as Knower-of-the-Field,
The Divine, in every being;
Discerning the Field from its Knower,
I consider – Wisdom Supreme. [2]

Now listen, I'll briefly describe
The Field, its nature and facets;
As well as the Knower-of-the-Field
In all of its various aspects. [3]

Sages of yore sung of these truths,
Deep wisdom their parables wield;
Indicating the Absolute,
The Divine, Knower-of-the-Field. [4]

The Field is the Body-and-Mind, O Prince
It comprises of Nature's Elements,
Of action-organs, senses, sense-objects,
Governed by ego, mind and intellect. [5]

Likes and dislikes, pleasure and pain,
And all aspects of the body;
Firm awareness and fortitude,
These are Field's facets and causes. [6]

As for Wisdom, I tell you: be humble, be honest,
Injure no creature, be forbearing to all;
Be pure, steadfast, serve your Teacher devoutly,
Be unpretentious, cultivate self control. [7]

Free from any egoism,
Senses – from constant craving, free;
Aware of human flawed clinging,
To birth, old age, death and misery. [8]

Reject not, nor identify with
Your loved one, children, and the rest;
Even-minded when attaining
Things the senses enjoy or detest. [9]

Avoid crowd's vain commotion,
Seeking solitude in its stead;
Devoted, unite fully with Me
As rivers merge with the sea. [10]

Aspire to know Inner-Self, and
Know clearly why it should be sought;
These are the roots of true Wisdom,
Darkness is merely opposed traits and thoughts.

|

These qualities mark true Wisdom,
And lead one – Wisdom to attain;
Know that they only bloom fully
In one who's by Wisdom – ordained. [11]

Now I'll describe That-to-be-Realized,
The Divine, Knower-of-the-Field;
Realizing it – is Wisdom,
Immortality – it wields. [12]

Beginning-less, beyond what isn't and is,
Permeates the whole world, in all it exists;
It is That which drives the world,
And That which Witnesses it. [12-13]

It is the ear within your ear,
The eye within – that truly sees;
Sense-less, devoid of Nature's-Facets,
Yet, That which enjoys all of these. [14]

So near and far away – is That,
Within, without – all life, all things;
So subtle – it is unknowable,
To the Wise – the core of one's being. [15]

Its Unity – undivided,
Yet appears split – to objects and beings;
From It, as dream figures, all stem,
To It they dissolve back again. [16]

This luminous Light of all lights,
Is beyond our Ignorance dark;
Wisdom and the Field's-Knower
Are ever in everyone's heart.

|

For as Wisdom dawns, Prince, you find,
You're not the Field, body or mind;
Then trying to observe the Observer too,
You suddenly Realize – the Knower is You! [17]

The Field, it's Knower and Wisdom,
Have hereby been briefly defined;
When one knows these one's ready for
Selfless union with the Divine. [18]

Know that Matter and Spirit are
Timeless, aspects of the Divine;
Three Nature's-Facets and their changes,
Emanate from Matter – we find. [19]

Matter, or Nature, is source of
All deeds and fruits of all action;
'Tis Spirit, or Soul, which 'feels' these
And undergoes pleasure or pain. [20]

The Soul, though it is the Divine,
In Body, in Nature – it dwells;
'This body I am' – errs the Soul,
And thus, Nature's-Facets – it 'feels'.

|

In Soul's mistaken identity,
Pleasures of Nature's-Facets it craves;
Spinning Birth-and-Death's endless wheel,
To this cyclic Samsara – enslaved. [21]

Beyond these is the Supreme-Soul,
Marred not by dullness or passions;
It is the Witness, Inner-Self,
Divine, empowering our actions. [22]

Matter, Spirit and Nature's-Facets,
One who knows all these as Divine;
Shall never again be born, Prince,
Be one's conduct coarse or refined. [23]

Some experience the Inner-Self
By themselves, in silent meditation;
Some adhere to the Wisdom Path,
Others take the Path of Action. [24]

Others must rely on hearsay
For they know not these noble paths;
If their faith be unshakable
They too, in time, cross beyond death. [25]

Know this, O Prince, Field and its Knower
Due to Ignorance – seem to be one;
All life and all lifeless – stem from
Confusing Nature with the Divine. [26]

One truly Sees, who sees the Lord
Abiding equally in every being;
That which is un-perishable
Within those that are decaying. [27]

Always aware of the good Lord
Dwelling in all beings around;
To whom can one offer anger?
For in all – but one's own Self is found. [28]

One truly Sees, who sees all action
Performed by Nature alone;
Knowing that Inner-Self acts not,
Highest truth – one has thus known. [29]

When one perceives all life forms
As united in the Divine,
Sees them from Divine emanating;
One then becomes – the Divine. [30]

Inner-Self is timeless, O Prince,
Devoid of any Nature-Trait;
Acts not, though it dwells in body,
Nor by action-fruits – can it taint. [31]

Even as space, all pervading,
Is so subtle – it's tainted-not;
So, Inner-Self, though embodied,
Is not stained by action or thought. [32]

Just as the entire world, Prince,
From the one sun receives its light;
So does the Knower, Inner-Self,
Light up the Field – ever so bright. [33]

Those who discern Field from Knower,
Through their inner eye of Wisdom;
Enter the Highest, Goal Supreme,
From Nature – they attain Freedom. [34]

"IN THE MORNING I BATHE MY INTELLECT IN
THE STUPENDOUS PHILOSOPHY OF THE GITA,
IN COMPARISON WITH WHICH OUR MODERN
WORLD AND ITS LITERATURE SEEM PUNY AND
TRIVIAL, OUR SHAKESPEARE SEEMS SOMETIMES
YOUTHFULLY GREEN."
—

Henry David Thoreau

Chapter fourteen further explores the 'mechanics' of the mind. All actions, thoughts and emotions – says the Gita – are driven by three 'Facets' of Nature: Pure, Active, and Dull. Like tinted eyeglasses, they taint your perception of the world around you, and your re-action to it. Purity is like a crystal clear lens; when it prevails you are attuned to your higher, Divine nature, and experience serene, selfless thoughts. When Activeness is dominant, your thinking is tainted by an agitated state of mind, and feelings of anger, desire and jealousy may arise. And when Dullness is dominant, you experience the world through totally dark lenses – you feel tired, your clarity is obscured, and your thinking is cloudy and perverted. Cultivating awareness to the workings of these Nature Facets, is a powerful key for inner-growth. It empowers you to realize that thoughts and emotions arising in you, are merely waves arising in the ocean of consciousness, whipped up by these three Facets of nature. And it encourages you to seek to enhance Purity in your life: "When through body's gates, all senses — Wisdom's clear light illumines and shines; then you know Purity is present — and in all you behold the Divine."

CHAPTER FOURTEEN

Nature's Three Facets

MASTER:

Once more, let Me declare to you,
The ultimate Wisdom of Mine;
Through it, the Wise reach My Unity,
When leaving their body behind. [1,2]

Mother Nature, enormous womb,
I, the Divine, inseminate;
And so, all creation's life-forms,
Spring forth, O Prince, and animate. [3]

Countless are the wombs of creation,
Delivering life's manifold forms;
I, Divine – the seed-giving father,
Mother Nature – womb of all wombs. [4]

Purity, Activeness, Dullness,
Nature's three Facets – from Her enmesh;
These are the chains that imprison
The Immortal, the Dweller in flesh. [5]

TYPES OF BONDS:
Purity, all illumining,
Will unveil your Inner-Self, Prince;
But so will Purity bind you,
To yearning for Wisdom and Bliss. [6]

Activeness, driven by passion,
Thirsts for pleasures and possession;
Activeness binds you, O Prince,
To endless hunger for action. [7]

Dullness, from Ignorance derived,
Enwraps all in thick confusion;
Dullness will bind and shackle you,
In bonds of sluggish illusion. [8]

Purity binds the contented,
Activeness binds men of action;
But Dullness, O Prince, binds the fools,
In opaque veils of distraction. [9]

Intertwined, these three Facets drive all,
Our every action, thought and gaze;
Purity is like a flame's clear light,
Dullness – its dark smoke, Activeness – its blaze.
|
At times, Purity shines, Prince,
Dullness and Activeness – it dispels;
At times Activeness dominates,
At other times Dullness prevails. [10]

When through body's gates, all senses,
Wisdom's clear light illumines and shines;
Then you know – Purity is present,
And in all you behold – the Divine. [11]

In heated action and in greed,
In restlessness, in all passion;
Know that Activeness rules, O Prince,
Fueling desires and action. [12]

And when mind is sluggish, inert,
Lethargic, fraught with confusion;
Know then that dark Dullness prevails
Heedlessly lost in illusion. [13]

TYPES OF DEATH:
One who meets death, leaves body,
When Purity prevails the mind;
Reaches the heavenly realms of
Knowers of the Highest, Divine. [14]

Those dying when Activeness rules,
Are born again here, action bound;
Those in Dullness – dull-witted are born
Among man or beast to be found. [15]

ACTION'S FRUITS:

Good action's fruits are Purity,
Wisdom Supreme, the purest joy;
Acts of Activeness – yield only pain,
Dullness acts – but Ignorance gain. [16]

From Purity – Wisdom is born,
From Activeness stems only greed;
Dullness begets but Ignorance,
Which to callous heedlessness leads. [17]

Those Pure – rise to high realms,
Men of Action – are here born again;
Those of Dullness, their lower nature,
To the nether worlds will descend. [18]

One who knows that all actions are
Performed by Nature's-Facets alone;
And knows That which is beyond them,
That, Divine, one's attained, has known. [19]

When the Dweller in body transcends
Nature's-Facets, from which the body's composed;
One's freed from pain, old age and death
To immortality transposed. [20]

PRINCE:

What marks one who has, O Master,
Gone beyond these three Nature-Traits?
How does one transcend them, pray tell,
How does such a Sage live and act? [21]

MASTER:

Hates not Purity, Activeness, Dullness,
Nor craves them when they're gone;
Therefore, O Prince, it is said that
Nature's-Facets – one has gone beyond. [22]

Sitting like one who's undisturbed,
By Nature's-Facets – disquieted not,
For, ever discerning, one knows:
All actions – but they carry out. [23]

Rests within, in Inner-Self's peace,
Earth, stone and gold – regarded the same;
Equally views those dear, those aloof ,
Praise and rebuke, pleasure and pain. [24]

To honor and shame, friend and foe,
Even minded, the same one responds;
Craves nothing, desires no action,
Nature's-Facets – one has crossed beyond. [25]

And one who is devoted to Me,
With all one's heart, soul and mind;
Thus crosses beyond Nature's-Facets,
Fit for union with Me, the Divine. [26]

For I am the Divine, Inner-Self,
In every being – large and minute;
Immortal, unchanging – I Am,
Existence-Knowledge-Bliss Absolute. [27]

Chapter fifteen provides a beautiful analogy to describe the
supreme Reality that we seek to know. Our human condition, or Samsara – says the Gita – may be likened to an
illusory 'upside-down' tree. It's roots up in heaven,
its vast branches spreading downwards to earth,
representing all our actions. All the world's sights,
sounds and other sense-stimuli, are like 'buds' of
this tree. From them grow the 'branches' of our actions, nourished and tainted by Nature's-Facets, described
in the previous chapter. This 'tree', and our human condition
of bondage and suffering – seem so formidably solid, yet they
are merely an illusion. They are instantly severed by the 'axe' of
non-attachment: Once ego stops fueling your actions, when
you no longer act motivated by what you 'like' and 'dislike',
then this 'tree' of bondage is no more. Carl Jung, referred
to this analogy in the Gita, and advises us: "who looks
outside dreams; who looks inside awakes". Such awakening is the culmination of Gita's Wisdom path:
"Desires gone, no more pride or delusion —
free from opposite-pairs, pleasure 'n pain;
Attachment quelled, firm in Inner-Self
they dwell — the Divine, timeless
goal, the Wise thus attain."

Reality Supreme

MASTER:
The wise speak symbolically of
Samsara's Impermanence-Tree;
Its roots up in heaven, Divine,
Limbs branching to Earth, intertwined.
|
Leaves of this tree – verses and hymns
Of all the Scriptures of Wisdom;
Knowing it truly, root and bough,
One has known – all there is to know. [1]

Upwards and down spread its branches,
Which Nature's-Facets feed and sustain;
Its buds – sense-objects, sights 'n sounds,
Its branches – spawn all deeds of men. [2]

Formidably deep seem its roots
Yet it exists not, what wonder!
The sharpened axe of non-attachment
Instantly cuts it asunder. [3]

Then, Samsara Tree felled, seek That
From which one returns not again;
Refuge you'll find in That Divine
From which this great Illusion began. [4]

Desires gone, no more pride or delusion,
Free from opposite-pairs, pleasure 'n pain;
Attachment quelled, firm in Inner-Self they dwell,
The Divine, timeless goal, the Wise thus attain. [5]

This is My infinite Being,
Attaining it – one's not reborn;
Self luminous ever so bright,
Shall sun, moon or fire – lend it light? [6]

A 'part' of Me dwells in Nature,
The essence of Soul in every being;
Congregating mind and five senses
In garment of flesh, bone and skin. [7]

When the Soul thus takes on a body
And at death – sheds it behind;
As wind carries scents of a flower
So does Soul carry senses and mind. [8]

Witnessing, presiding over
Mind, eyes 'n ears, touch, taste 'n smell;
Sole enjoyer of all sense-objects,
On which mind constantly dwells. [9]

Dwelling in flesh and enjoying
Or leaving this body behind;
The Wise' behold this Inner-Self,
The Ignorant – to its presence are blind. [10]

Yogis striving – behold the Divine,
They know certain: 'That – I Am';
But those lacking calm discernment,
This Wisdom – they cannot attain. [11]

Mine is the Light-of-Consciousness,
The essence and source of all light;
It shines pure in fire, moon and sun,
Illumines the world – ever so bright. [12]

Vitality-Essence of Mine,
Pulsates, upholds all creation;
My Moisture-Essence, life's-sap,
Its nourishment and its hydration. [13]

My Vital-Air, breath's bellows in all,
Kindles Digestive-Fire that's Mine;
In truth every morsel eaten is
Consumed by Me, the Divine. [14]

I, the Divine, dwell in all hearts,
Memory, knowledge, from Me both stem;
I am the truths of all Scriptures,
And Vedanta – Knowledge Supreme. [15]

There are two types of beings in this world:
The perishing, and that which perishes not;
Perishing – all beings of the visible world,
Un-perished – Creation's-Illusion, their source. [16]

But beyond and separate from these
There exists Inner-Self Supreme;
It is the Abstract, Eternal Lord,
Sustains all worlds, dwells in all beings. [17]

I, Inner-Self, am beyond the perishing,
Samsara's symbolic Impermanence Tree;
The Imperishable – I also transcend,
Hence I am known as Reality Supreme. [18]

One who is free from Illusion
And knows Me – Reality Supreme;
Knows all there is to know, O Prince,
Worships Me – with one's whole being. [19]

This is the most secret science I've taught you,
Knowing it, O Prince, one becomes truly Wise;
One's life-goal attained, duties accomplished,
From timeless oblivion one now opens one's eyes. [20]

"THE BHAGAVAD GITA IS A VERY IMPORTANT
MAP FOR UNDERSTANDING THE NATURE OF
CONSCIOUSNESS"
—

Deepak Chopra

PREFACE TO CHAPTER SIXTEEN

Chapter sixteen describes the 'battlefield' of our soul, between our higher and lower tendencies. A battlefield, which is more pronounced in our troubled times, perhaps like never before. There are two tendencies in human nature – says the Gita – our higher, Divine nature, and our lower, primal one. The 'lotus' in you, and the 'mud' from which it arises. These tendencies are so polarly different, that it's almost as though they represent different types of beings altogether. Gita's description of lower tendencies is jarring: "'This I wanted, I got it today — that other, tomorrow I'll own; All these vast riches are mine now — I'll grab all the rest very soon'". It doesn't require us much imagination to think of persons that seem to fit that description well. "'I am so rich and distinguished — who in the world would compare?' Deluded, thus the Ignorant think — 'I'll enjoy life, donate, attend prayer.'" Unfortunately, it is a fair description of the ailments of our society and norms. More importantly though, it is an invitation to boldly look inside yourself, and to identify these very same tendencies, even if more subtle – in your own behavior. Once you do that, you are well on your way to set out to correct them.

CHAPTER SIXTEEN

Divine and Lower Tendencies

MASTER:
A person born higher-nature inclined,
Is pure of heart and knows no fear;
Steadfast in Wisdom and Yoga,
Is generous, direct and sincere.
|

Practices Self-Discipline,
Holding senses under tight rein;
Prays and studies the Scriptures,
Union-Divine – is keen to attain. [1]

Harms no creature, in thought or deed,
Truthful, speaks words that don't injure;
Renounced, forthright, ever serene,
Free of desire and anger.
|

Gentle, modest, caring to all,
From useless commotion refrains;
No longer given to greed, O Prince,
And when erring – feels shame. [2]

Vital, resilient, pure-minded,
Trusts one's divine inner-strength;
Forgiving, free from hatred and pride,
– These are one's natural born traits. [3]

One who's lower-nature disposed,
Is given to rage and conceit;
Born an ignorant, hypocrite,
Is arrogant and cruel to the weak. [4]

Divine inclination – breeds freedom,
Bondage – by lower-nature is spawned;
But fear not, O Prince, for by birth
Your nature's divinely-inclined. [5]

There are two types of beings in this world,
Some driven by lower-nature, others by the
Divine; Those of higher-nature I've told you about,
Now let me describe the lower-natured ones. [6]

Those driven by lower-nature
Know not what to do, what to shun;
They've no purity, no right conduct,
Nor is truth – in them to be found. [7]

"The Scriptures are but lies" – they say,
"There is no god, no moral law;
The world is caused by sex and lust" –
They know no truth, they feel no awe. [8]

And since these poor bewildered souls
Believe this in their confused dark minds;
They carry out horrible deeds,
Foes of the world and of mankind. [9]

Minds filled with endless desires,
These arrogant, prideful drunk souls;
In blindness – run after evil,
Intent on gaining impure goals. [10]

And so, they evoke countless worries,
From which only death sets them free;
Fulfillment of lusts is their highest aim,
Thinking that's all life can be. [11]

A hundred ties of anxious hope
Bind them, begetting lust and rage;
Striving to gain sensual pleasures,
They hoard wealth, in devious ways. [12]

"This I wanted – I got it today,
That other – tomorrow I'll own;
All these vast riches are mine now,
I'll grab all the rest – very soon." [13]

"This rival – I've now defeated,
All others will soon yield to me;
I rule, I enjoy life's pleasures,
I'm so perfect, so strong and carefree." [14]

"I am so rich, and distinguished,
Who in the world would compare?"
- Deluded, thus the Ignorant think -
"I'll enjoy life, donate, attend prayer". [15]

To sensual pleasures – addicted,
Restless, from mind's countless desires;
Trapped in Illusion's web, they fall
To the hell of their mind's foul mire. [16]

They're self conceited and stubborn,
Their wealth – an intoxication;
All their donations and prayers
Aren't heartfelt, but mere ostentation. [17]

Driven by ego, hungry for power, they're
Lustful and angry, malicious and vain;
In their own body and in all others, My
Presence, Divine, they deny and disdain. [18]

Humanity's worst enemies,
Savage haters, worst among men;
To wombs of degraded parents,
I cast them again and again. [19]

From these lowly births, degraded,
Birth after birth, lower they fall;
Me, the Divine, they attain not,
Reach the lowest state of the soul. [20]

Three gateways lead to this hell, O Prince,
To man's destruction they lead;
One must therefore abandon these three
Lust, anger and greed. [21]

One, Liberated, who passes by
These three gateways to darkness;
Persisting in one's practices,
In time attains to God's oneness. [22]

But one who's enslaved by desires,
Casting aside Scriptures' decrees;
Attains no perfection, O Prince,
Nor happiness – Wisdom that frees. [23]

Therefore, let the Scriptures guide you
What shouldn't be done and what should;
Study the Scriptures' Action Path,
Then act in this world as you would. [24]

Chapter seventeen returns to discuss Nature's Facets, and the
insights they provide on our inner journey. Which path I
should take, asks the Prince. Which faith, which spiritual practice are best? What's the best form of charity? The best diet? None of these is best – says
the Gita – there is no 'one best' faith or spiritual practice. If indeed you seek to 'scale the sum-
mit' of Inner-Self, then carefully observe the workings
of Nature's three Facets, in your mind and your actions.
Such close observation of how your mind works – is not always pleasant. Observe and you will see, that in all things in
your life there is an admixture of the workings of the three
Nature Facets, these 'tinted-glasses' of the mind. 'Spiritual' practices are no exception. They too may be pure, or
might be selfish, depending on your underlying motivation.
Gita's verses gently, lovingly guide you, how to carefully discern the motivations that underly and drive
your actions, and then do your best to purify them:
"A Pure gift is one that's given to — one worthy, at the right time and place; Not for past
favors, or in order to receive — the
giver just knows: 'I need to give'."

CHAPTER SEVENTEEN

Three Kinds of Faith

PRINCE:

Some people pray, faithful at heart,
Though not quite according to Scripture;
Of what Nature-Facet is their faith,
Is it Dull, Active or Pure? [1]

MASTER:

Faith of mortals is of three types,
By one's dominant Nature-Trait;
Whether it's Pure, Active, or Dull,
Listen, Prince – I will elaborate. [2]

One's faith, O Prince, is in accord
With one's disposition – we find;
For one's faith ever permeates
All thoughts within one's mind. [3]

TYPES OF FAITH:

Those Pure of heart – worship God,
Power and riches – the Active revere;
The rest, Dull-natured, deluded,
Spirits 'n ghosts they worship and fear. [4]

Know that those who torment the body,
Beyond what the Scriptures decree;
Are driven by their attachment,
Their ego, lust and hypocrisy. [5]

Foolish, they weaken the body,
Vex Me, Divine – within it I dwell;
Know, O Prince, that such foolishness
Is by lower-nature – propelled. [6]

Likewise, Food is of three types,
As are Worship and Discipline;
Listen, I'll tell you about these,
And of the three types of Giving. [7]

TYPES OF FOOD:

Pure foods are fresh, light and nourishing,
Appetizing, tasty, sweet, juicy and wholesome;
Such foods soothe and strengthen mind and body,
Bestow cheerfulness, inner-quiet and calm. [8]

The Active take hot, spicy foods,
Eat meat, and drink coffee and wine;
Such foods harm body's health balance,
Stirring lust, disquieting the mind. [9]

The Dull-natured smoke drugs and eat
Overcooked food that's tasteless, impure;
These tire and plunder body's vigor,
Mind's clarity – they obscure. [10]

TYPES OF WORSHIP:

God's worship, not craving reward,
Is the worship of Purity;
In line with Scriptures' injunctions,
Driven by firm inner-duty. [11]

Those who worship craving reward,
Their vain ostentation upheld;
Know this, Prince, those who pray thusly
By Activeness Facet are impelled. [12]

Contrary to Scriptures' edicts,
Is the worship born of Dullness;
Revering not God nor Teachers,
Holy rites disregarded, faithless. [13]

TYPES OF DISCIPLINE:
Worshipping God and Masters revered,
Non-violence, purity and honesty;
Sexual desires controlled, not repressed,
These are Self-Discipline of Body. [14]

Speaking without ever causing pain,
Truthful words that console and reach;
Constant study of the Scriptures,
These are Self-Discipline of Speech. [15]

Serenity, silence, pure motives,
To all creatures – being kind;
Mental control, meditation,
These are Self-Discipline of Mind. [16]

Self-Discipline of body, speech and mind,
Practiced steadfast, devoutly;
Desiring no rewards, O Prince,
Is Self-Discipline of Purity. [17]

Feigned Self-Discipline that's practiced
Wishing to gain fame and respect;
Is Activeness' Self-Discipline,
Unstable it is, and transient. [18]

Self inflicted body torture
Or acts meant to cause others pain;
Are Self-Discipline of Dullness,
No benefit can these attain. [19]

TYPES OF GIFTS:

A Pure gift is one that's given to
One worthy, at the right time and place;
Not for past favors, or in order to receive,
The giver just knows: "I need to give". [20]

Gift given for selfish motives,
Reluctantly, or for acclaim;
Is a gift born of Activeness,
'Tis given in order to gain. [21]

Gift given to one unworthy,
At the wrong time and the wrong place;
Insensitive to recipient's feelings,
Is a gift of Dullness, O Prince. [22]

Om-Tat-Sat, this three-fold Mantra,
Stands for 'the Divine', the world's source;
Scriptures, Sages and holy rites, from
These sacred sounds were all formed. [23]

Devotees incant Om, or Amen,
For it denotes the Divine;
Whenever they act, give or pray,
United in It – heart and mind. [24]

Liberty seekers intone Tat,
Expect not fruit of their action;
They know – That, indestructible,
Alone carries out all acting. [25]

The sound Sat – stands for Reality,
Indivisible, Infinite, Eternal;
It reminds us – Divine alone Is,
All other notions – Unreal. [26]

Every action, though imperfect,
Pledged selflessly – to the Divine;
Is Sat, or Real, it draws one near,
To that One Reality Sublime. [27]

But faithless actions, prayers and gifts,
Faithless Self-Disciplines too;
Are false, are 'That which is not', O Prince,
Here and Hereafter no good will they do. [28]

"Yes, I am a Hindu. I am also a Christian, a Muslim, a Buddhist and a Jew."

"When doubts haunt me, when disappointments stare me in the face, and when I see not one ray of light on the horizon, I turn to the Gita, and find a verse to comfort me. And immediately, in the midst of overwhelming sorrow I begin to smile."

—

Mahatma Gandhi

PREFACE TO CHAPTER EIGHTEEN

Our Gita journey is coming to a close. We've followed the
Prince through Gita's three paths – of Action, Devotion and
Wisdom. From his initial cry for help, to his triumphant
cry of awakening. Chapter eighteen concludes the
Gita, recapping and integrating its three paths. But
rather than being an ending, it is an invitation to
start over again! And like a magic spiral stairway, as
you read and re-read this simple, profound discourse –
it keeps lifting you up higher every time round. In the footsteps of giants before you, you're invited to this 'alchemy'
of the Gita. It's timeless words of Wisdom empower you to
do good in the world, and to be transformed in the process.
We all seek happiness in our various ways. You start your
journey, looking for it outside, and expecting 'quick fixes'.
Gita's way, of training your mind, requires perseverance,
and feels difficult, and 'bitter' at first. Of the many Wis-
dom-pearls of chapter eighteen, perhaps this one,
which defines happiness, captures the essence
of the Gita: "Only one who knows Inner-Self
— knows true happiness, happiness Pure;
Bitter first, but then, lo what sweetness
— from Illusion's sorrow the cure."

Liberation Through Renunciation

PRINCE:

I desire to know these two,
Detachment and Renunciation;
What is the difference between these,
O Master, would you, please explain? [1]

MASTER:

Giving up desire-driven acts,
We are told – is renunciation;
Detachment, say sages of yore,
Is renouncing the fruits of action. [2]

There's bad in all action – some say,
From all action one should refrain;
Others say one shouldn't reject acts of
Giving, prayer and Self-Discipline. [3]

The truth about Renunciation,
Pray listen, and you will find;
Renunciation too, O Prince,
Is indeed of three different kinds. [4]

One must not discontinue
Giving, Self-Discipline and prayers;
For the Wise who understand these
They are potent purifiers. [5]

But even these must be performed
Desiring not fruits of action;
Rather leaving attachment behind,
This is my doubtless conviction. [6]

TYPES OF RENUNCIATION:

When one idles from upholding,
One's natural Duty, O Prince;
Dull is such renunciation
And rooted in dark Ignorance. [7]

Refraining from actions unpleasant
Or from those that might lead to pain:
Is renunciation of Activeness,
Leads not to any true gain. [8]

But when one's Duty is performed
Merely because – do it one ought;
Pure is such renunciation,
Detached, O Prince, craving not. [9]

True renunciate, pure of heart,
Whose inner light cuts doubts asunder;
Does not shirk the unpleasant,
Nor after the pleasant – hanker. [10]

Verily, mortals, embodied,
Their actions – cannot fully negate;
But one who gives up action's fruit,
Is deemed a true renunciate. [11]

Those clinging to ego's cravings, their
Actions bear fruits – good, bad and mixed;
But actions of the egoless,
Bear no fruit – in this world or the next. [12]

Inner-Self is but a Witness,
Our actions are caused by these five,
We're taught by Yoga's wisdom,
To free us from Bonds-of-Action. [13]

First – this body, second – ego,
The sense organs, and life forces;
And also the spirit that presides
Over each of these senses. [14]

Every action man undertakes,
These five always act it – we find;
Be it a noble act, be it wicked,
Whether in body, speech or mind. [15]

Thus, undiscerning is one who
Thinks oneSelf – the doer of action;
Unrefined is such mind, still untrained,
OneSelf for body – mistaken. [16]

But one who's ever free from ego,
Mind not tainted by virtue or sin;
Kills not, is not bound by action,
Though his hand – strikes all these men. [17]

Hear now of the different types of
Knowledge, Action and Doer;
Each of these too is of three types
By their Facet – Dull, Active, or Pure. [18,19]

TYPES OF KNOWLEDGE:

Purity's Knowledge – is Wisdom,
Which knows but one Reality;
Immutable, dwells in all beings,
Within all divisions – Unity. [20]

The knowledge of Activeness, though,
Knows only differentiation;
Separate souls, in disparate bodies,
Distinction and separation. [21]

Distorted and irrational
Is the dark 'knowledge' of Dullness;
Mistaking a part for the whole,
Unaware of nature's oneness. [22]

TYPES OF ACTIONS:

Act of sacred Duty, unattached,
Without dislike or desire;
By one who wishes no reward,
Such action is said to be Pure. [23]

Act of weary exertion,
Driven by ego, roused by desire;
Is an act of the Activeness Facet,
Performed despiteful of nature. [24]

An act of reckless abandon,
Of one's abilities – heedless;
Deluded, insensitive, squandering,
Is an action of Dullness. [25]

TYPES OF DOERS:
One who egoless, acts unattached,
By victory or failure – not swayed;
Avid, persevering, steadfast,
Is a person of Nature's Pure Trait. [26]

One lustful, craving vainglory,
Quick to rejoice, quick to despair;
Is a person driven by Activeness,
Brutal, impure and unfair. [27]

Lazy, loitering, cheating,
Indifferent, heart's not in one's deed;
Stubborn, desponding, malicious;
Such person the Dullness Facet breeds. [28]

Likewise there are three different types of
Awareness and Determination;
By their dominant Nature-Facet
I'll clearly describe them – now listen. [29]

TYPES OF AWARENESS:
Awareness that's Pure, clearly discerns,
Ego-identification;
From the path of non-attachment,
Which leads one to liberation.
|
Thus it knows fear 'n fearlessness' source,
What oughtn't be done, and what ought;
What binds the embodied spirit, and
What leads to the Freedom it sought. [30]

Active Facet's Awareness
Discerns not what's right from what's wrong;
That which one ought to do, O Prince,
From actions which one ought to shun. [31]

Thick veils of Ignorance enshroud,
Awareness of Dull Nature-Trait;
Distorted, it takes right for wrong,
Sees all things perverted, none straight. [32]

TYPES OF RESOLVE:
Pure Resolve – is firm, never falters,
By practice of Yoga – is gained;
For vitality, mind and senses,
Through this practice are all restrained. [33]

Desire-driven Resolve is that which
By Activeness Facet – is spawned;
It lusts pleasure, wealth and reward
For natural duties performed. [34]

Dull Resolve – is but stubbornness
Of a fool who's clinging on tight;
To sorrow, despair and slumber,
To one's conceit and one's fright. [35]

Now listen, and
I'll tell you, Prince;
Of the three types
Of happiness. [36]

TYPES OF HAPPINESS:
Only one who knows Inner-Self
Know true happiness – happiness Pure;
Bitter first, but then lo what sweetness,
From Illusion's sorrow – the cure. [37]

Senses delight in contacting their
Sense-objects – scent, sound and sight;
Sweet first, yet at last – so bitter,
But poison – is Activeness' delight. [38]

From Dullness arises crude joy,
Of sleepy, heedless confusion;
Its beginning, its end – both are
Indolent, slothful delusion. [39]

There isn't a creature on earth,
Nor deity in heaven above;
Free from these three Nature-Facets,
Which from Matter, Nature – derive. [40]

Seer, Leader, Merchant, Servant,
Members of each social class;
To each – their natural-born Calling,
Caused by Nature-Traits and by deeds past. [41]

Seers, Pure-natured, their Calling is
To know their own Inner-Self, Divine;
Honest, renounced, controlled, seek Wisdom,
Tolerant, firm-of-faith, serene-mind. [42]

Leaders – Pure and Active natured,
Their Calling's to be skillful and bold;
Be firm, generous, rule justly,
These are their tendencies-born. [43]

Some are born to provide others' needs,
These are Merchants – Active their Trait;
Others, Servants – born Dull and Active,
And to serve all is their fate. [44]

To each one, each one – their Calling,
Through it, perfection is attained;
Hear now, how perfection is reached,
By pursuing one's Calling ordained. [45]

You reach perfection if but,
Your Calling's Duty you do – as prayer;
To that all pervasive Divine,
Sole Doer, in truth, everywhere. [46]

Better imperfectly follow your Calling,
Than perfectly tackle another's instead;
Your natural born Calling, pursued unattached,
Bears no sin, regardless of what life one's led. [47]

Therefore forsake not your Calling's-Duty,
Even if not perfectly done;
For action's always imperfect,
As fire by smoke will be bound. [48]

One whose mind is ever unattached,
Who's freed from desire, is self-restrained;
Freedom from action, the Supreme State,
Through renunciation one quickly attains. [49]

Learn from Me now, in brief, O Prince,
How one who's attained perfection;
Reaches that goal, Wisdom Supreme,
Through total devotion to Wisdom. [50]

When senses are firmly restrained,
Mind, disillusioned, rests in the Divine;
When sight, taste 'n sound are abandoned,
Without attraction, repulsion, [51]

When one seeks solitude, silence,
Eats little, curbs speech, body, mind;
When one cultivates dispassion,
And ever meditates on the Divine, [52]

When one sheds vanity, violence,
Pride, lust, anger, notion of 'mine';
Free from ego, serene at heart,
One's ready – for Union Divine. [53]

United thus, in the Divine,
In Inner-Self – dwelling serene;
Grieves not, craves not, feels for all,
To Me, Divine – devoted supreme. [54]

Devotion leads to Wisdom, Prince,
Devotion to Me – to Wisdom Supreme;
Truly thus knowing Me, Divine,
No longer mortal, one enters My being. [55]

The Wise thus performs all actions,
Ever submitting to Me, Divine;
Through My divine Grace, O Prince,
Divine, highest state, one thus finds. [56]

Mentally renounce all your actions
To Me, your Beloved, Divine;
Harness your discrimination,
On Me – ever fixed, heart and mind. [57]

Mind fixed thus on Me, Divine,
By My Grace all hardships you'll conquer;
But if vainly you heed Me not,
Why, surely, O Prince – you are lost. [58]

If prideful you state "I shan't fight",
In vain is your resolve, your prattle;
Your very own nature itself
Is that which will drive you to battle. [59]

Action-Bonds, Karma, that shackle you,
You yourself have fastened in the past;
Your Ignorance opposes in vain,
Deeds which you will do at last. [60]

Think not God is distant, O Prince,
In the hearts of all beings He dwells;
Round and round, He whirls them all on
His Creation's-Illusion spinning wheel. [61]

Seek refuge in Him, wholehearted,
For He dwells in your own heart, within;
Ignorance – forever dispelled,
Through His Grace, you'll find Peace Supreme. [62]

This Wisdom, secret of secrets,
With you, O Prince, I have now shared;
Think it over, carefully, reflect,
Then as you see fit – go and act. [63]

The most profound of all truths,
Pray listen, I will tell you again;
I speak for your own good, O Prince,
You're My beloved disciple and friend. [64]

Give Me your heart, O Prince, love and adore Me,
Worship Me always, bow down only to Me;
Then you shall find Me, that is My promise,
For you are the one who is so dear to Me. [65]

Let your duties be done through you
By a mightier hand, Divine;
Take refuge in Me, grieve no more,
I'll save you from bondage and sin. [66]

Never share these truths, O Prince,
With one not desiring to learn;
Undisciplined, and irreverent
To one's teacher or Me, the Divine. [67]

But one who teaches this Gita
To all my sincere devotees;
To Me, the Divine – purely devoted,
Surely, will come onto Me. [68]

Dearer service than this, O Prince,
No living soul can provide Me;
Nor do I, Divine, find here on Earth
One dearer than such devotee. [69]

And any one who meditates
On this, our discourse Divine;
Attains the highest perfection
For worshipping Me – heart and mind. [70]

Even if one but listens to it,
Pure faith in one's heart, and love;
From sins one's freed, and is seated
With the righteous – in heavens above. [71]

Have you listened, single-minded
To this, O Prince, my Wisdom lore?
Have all your doubts been dispelled,
Your Ignorance delusion – is no more? [72]

PRINCE:
Through your Grace, my Lord, my Master,
My mind stands firm, deluded no more;
True Wisdom – dispelled all my doubts,
I shall do your bidding, my Lord. [73]

These are the words that moved my heart,
This wondrous discourse, Yoga supreme,
From the lips of the high-souled Prince,
And those of the Master, Lord of all beings.

Time and again, I rejoice recalling
Sacred, inspiring truths
The Master taught his friend.

The resplendent form, which
The Master donned,
I reminisce time and again.

For, wherever the Master is
And greatest of archers, the Prince,
There, I know, is goodness
And victory, and glory and peace. [78]

Om. Peace. Peace. Peace.

EPILOGUE

I am seated in the shade, on a solitary Mediterranean beach. Emerald, shimmery waters, still lukewarm, but now a bit cooler every day. Summer is ending.

Thirty two years have passed since I first met the Gita, as a young medical student, merely looking to improve my Yoga teaching skills, and perhaps 'pick-up' some philosophy on the way. And twelve years since I started working in earnest on this translation. Earlier first drafts are overlaid by jolly, heavy-handed doodles of my daughter Maya – then an energetic toddler, enthusiastically 'helping' dad; now turning eighteen, and a trusted advisor to this book's artistic design.

This beach here, and the Gita, have seen me through these three decades of my life. Through great triumphs and dark tribulations; through heights of happiness and depths of despair; through career, relationships, marriage and parenting.

This much I know to be true: Gita's message is meant for ordinary people, like you and me, who are living in this hectic, troubled, beautiful world and time of ours. If you seek a practical, Wisdom-guide to facilitate your inner-journey, you're welcome to the Gita. I also know that Gita's lofty ideals are not at all exaggerated or utopian — I've had the incredible fortune to sit at the feet of Teachers, who for me are shining examples of Gita's principles in action. When you meet men and women like these, their humility and kindness melts your heart, and the clear light that flows through them enlightens your soul.

May we all continue to learn and evolve, and to help and support one another on our individual inner journeys, toward our own Inner-Self.

ABOUT THIS TRANSLATION

There are many fine translations of the Gita, focusing on various aspects of the text. The current translation views the Gita as a powerful, practical guide for inner development, and strives to make this aspect of the Gita accessible and relevant to modern readers.

Work on this translation progressed in a very slow, iterative manner, eventually spanning twelve years. It was a process which felt much like peeling layers of an onion: focusing on peeling one layer at a time, which then exposes, and sets the ground for peeling the layer underneath it. The amount of work I put in, and the progress made, varied at different periods. From long stretches of working many hours a day, to periods of only limited time invested, working around my 'day-job' commitments. Often being satisfied with working and meditating on just one or two verses a day.

In the first couple of years, I went through multiple iterations, simply trying to capture the essence of each verse, with an emphasis on its inner-development aspect. The following two years focused first on carefully removing distracting layers of complex terminology and foreign culture. As an example, to improve readability and simplicity, I replaced Sanskrit philosophical terms with English 'placeholders' that capture their essence: I let Atman – simply be your Inner-Self, which you journey to discover; Dharma

– is your life's Calling, to which you are advised to remain true; Maya – is Nature's-Veil, the visible world which hides, as though, its underlying divine Unity; and so forth. I've similarly let Arjuna and Krishna – simply be the Prince and the Master. Subsequent iterations were then devoted to carefully weave in wording, as needed, which clarify the meaning of each verse, based on classic commentaries of the Gita. This, so that the text can be read and be clearly understood by a contemporary reader who is not versed in these commentaries.

The following three years were focused on iterations of re-writing the text into basic poetic form, using a format of four lines per verse, which I found appealing; and subsequently adding partial rhyming. And so, by year seven, there was a good draft, which I was pretty happy with.

And then some magical things happened. Significant insights came up, as the Gita's practice and meditations became enmeshed in my life. Insights which thoroughly transformed the translation, and which filled the next five years of work on it.

First, I was pretty shocked to learn that the meter I was drawn to in my translation is in fact the exact meter of the original Sanskrit text. In my ignorance, I was initially unaware of this. Apparently, the vast majority of Gita's seven hundred Sanskrit verses are written in Shloka (or Anushtubh) meter – four lines of eight syllables; and a minority of verses are in Tristubh meter – four lines of eleven syllables. I then therefore started to slowly re-write the entire translation, this time strictly adhering to these two meters.

Then, as I was working on the doing so, I gradually became more aware of the verses' magical melodiousness. And so I started over, yet again, this time paying special attention to the music, crafting the wording to support it, and subtly relaxing the syllable count where appropriate. Gita's seven hundred verses have been likened to a string of pearls; I did my best to 'smooth' these 'pearls of wisdom', so that they harmoniously roll around in your mind, doing their work.

Subsequent iterations, over the final several years, included carefully revising the translation so that it speaks equally to women as it does to men; a deepening of the translation to incorporate insights made clearer through meditation and as expounded by the classic commentaries; a thorough re-editing, with a view to making the translation more accessible and relevant to a contemporary reader; and work on esthetic and typographic aspects of both the printed and electronic book formats.

Another major effort undertaken, was the compilation and integration of the original Sanskrit text of each verse, its literal translation, and a word-by-word translation. These were adapted, with permission, from Swami Shivananda's translation, and are made available on the book's website, at *www.newgita.com*; in the e-book version they are incorporated as hyperlinks. I did not incorporate these into the printed book, so as not to distract from the simplicity and poetic format, which I view as paramount. For those interested, these resources provide full granularity of the original text, and transparency into the translation considerations taken.

A 'Yoga Philosophy Basics' introductory section briefly defines Gita's key philosophical terms – I warmly recommend reading it first. In a few cases I have united, split or omitted verses, for clarity; these are all clearly marked. Similar to other translations, I omitted the first half of the first chapter, which is not part of Gita's dialogue and does not contribute much to its understanding.

I hope the above approaches taken help make the text accessible and helpful for your inner journey. For the text to be effective, remember to try and avoid over-intellec-tualization. Enjoy its beauty, and let its truth touch your heart, and its music stir your soul.

ABOUT THE AUTHOR

Isaac Bentwich M.D. is a longtime practitioner and teacher of Yoga and Meditation. He is also a Medical Doctor and scientist, who has founded three life-science technology companies, leading revolutions in medicine, genomics, and environment conservation. His work is featured in top-tier scientific and business publications.

In genomics, Dr. Bentwich and his colleagues analyzed the human genome, leading to a landmark discovery of hundreds of novel genes, based on which they delivered novel diagnostic tests, for patients of cancer and other diseases. In conservation, Dr. Bentwich and his team developed an agricultural technology that allows farmers to grow more crop using less water and other resources.

Dr. Bentwich received his Medical Doctor degree from Ben Gurion University, in Israel in 1989. He is also trained in Ayurvedic medicine, and in Yoga therapy.

The vision and innovations that underly each of the companies he founded and led, came through months of silent meditation retreats, in the Galilee and at the foothills of the Himalayas.

His work on this translation of the Gita has spanned twelve years.

To learn more about Dr. Bentwich's work, write him at *bentwich@newgita.com*, or visit *www.newgita.com*.

ACKNOWLEDGMENTS

Several prior translations of the Gita, classic Gita commentaries, and classic Vedanta philosophy texts greatly assisted this work; my deepest gratitude to their authors. These include: Christopher Isherwood and Swami Prahvananda's excellent Gita translation (1944); Shankara's classic Gita commentary and the Mandukya Upanishad and its commentaries. Of special mention is Swami Shivananda's Gita translation and commentary (1968), which includes an authoritative literal word-by-word translation of the original text, as well as an inspiring commentary, by a recognized spiritual master of our time.

I am grateful to my parents who are my first teachers. To my late mother who did not get to see this book, and who ever remains in my heart, a beacon of purity and goodness. And to my grandfather, Joseph Bentwich, whose spirit is with me wherever I go. I am ever indebted to my teachers, at whose feet I am blessed to sit, and who are for me living examples of the Gita's principles in action. The late Lama Kirti Tsenshab Rimpoche, whose humility and compassionate wisdom helped soften a callous heart. And my teacher and dear friend Brahmananda, without whom this book wouldn't be here, nor would I.

I am grateful to my wife and Love, Gefen, by whose love I am blessed and surrounded; to my children, Iddo, Maya and Itamar, from whom I continue to learn every day.

Many dear friends contributed significantly to this work; my deep, heartfelt gratitude to each an every one of them. Special thanks to my good friend, Phil Cousineau, whose wise advice helped shape and steer this book. To my brother David Bentwich, and daughter Maya Bentwich, for their indispensable 'artistic eye' and wise suggestions. To Nadav Shalev, who helped design the book, and bore with me patiently through its iterations. To Eileen Duhné, who helped get the book into hands of readers, no small feat. To Benny Carmy, who helped with masterful e-marketing.

Special thanks to my students over the years. Your questions inspired and enriched this book, and seeing the effect Gita's teachings had in your lives – energized the work on this translation and publication. And to my fellow Harmonia team members, who help enable this work.

Finally, I am grateful to you, the reader, for it is thanks to you, that I've had the great fortune of working on this translation. May this book bring as much joy and light into your life, as it has in mine.

COLOPHON

The Gita was designed by Isaac Bentwich and Nadav Shalev. The title was typeset in Optima, a stylized humanist sans-serif, developed in 1958 by visionary German typeface designer Hermann Zapf for Stempel AG foundry. Inspired by Renaissance stone carvings he saw while on vacation in Florence in 1950, he sketched a first draft on the back of a 1000 lira banknote, and went on to work on perfecting it for close to a decade. The body text and headings were typeset in Mercury Text, a family of spirited, subtle contemporary serif fonts, created in 1999 by Jonathan Hoefler and Tobias Frere-Jones for Hoefler&Co. Initially inspired by the Dutch baroque style of punchcutter Johann Michael Fleischman (1701-1768) – Mercury Text was developed over nine years, as a high-performance typeface, that thrives under demanding conditions of modern high-speed press. The commentary text sections were typeset in Absara Sans, a contemporary sans serif font, designed by French type designer Xavier Dupré for FontFont in 2005.

For more copies of *Gita – A Timeless Guide for Our Time*, or further information about the author's writing and workshops, please contact us at: *bentwich@newgita.com*

FURTHER STUDY

Study and practice of the Gita is a lifelong quest. Go beyond the book, enrich your reading experience of the Gita and its impact in your life:

Visit *www.newgita.com* for additional Gita teachings by the author, and other helpful resources, including online video classes, schedule of physical workshops, and support for Gita study groups. Also available there is online access to the full original Sanskrit text of each verse, its literal translation, and word-by-word translation.

* * *

Finally – if you would, I encourage you to please take a moment to briefly share your honest feedback on the book; this can be of great help to other prospective readers. You may do so on Amazon and/or GoodReads. This book is independently published, and is not backed by a big publisher, and so your help is much appreciated

CPSIA information can be obtained
at www.ICGtesting.com
Printed in the USA
BVHW03025310519
549838BV00005B/20/P